2 Cameras - 3 Wars
Korean War Edition

thru the lens of Rupy

To, M EL

THANK!

Photos and insights by:

Peter P Ruplenas

" Rupy "

2 Cameras, 3 Wars - Korean War Edition
Copyright © 2014 by Peter P Ruplenas

ISBN 66943

Printed in USA by 48HrBooks (www.48HrBooks.com)

Table of Contents

Foreword

Introduction

Korean War chapters

Foreward

As a United States Army Still Photographer, it has been my experience that many do not understand the mission of the Still Photographer/Combat Photographer, let alone realize that such a MOS designation has ever existed. The missions vary, but rarely are they as glamorous as many think. Soldiering and photographing at the same time is no easy thing when the bullets are flying. Anything is possible, from studio work, intel gathering, meet and greet type photos, to combat photography. The later is what Sgt Peter Ruplenas is known for.

It was at a church gathering on a late fall afternoon, with a nip in the air, I noticed an older gentleman sitting over by himself. Immediately I notice he was wearing a "veteran" ball cap, and as usually I just had to meet another American Hero. You see the love for the military is still in my blood. Those were some of the best years of my younger life.

As I introduced myself, and thanked this man for his service to me, my family and my country, I asked what his MOS was back in the day.............. "84C Combat Photographer," was Peters reply. I could not believe my ears, never before had I met another US Army Photographer, as we were a rare breed even when I had served. I was delighted, and my interest grew and my mind's eye could almost see the images that he described as he told account after account of his missions from the deep files of his mind,

like a movie reel, that played on and on.

This experience will be yours, but even greater as you relive past history through Sgt Ruplenas's eyes and camera, the various history changing events that many have either forgot or are not even aware of, and it brings tears to my eyes to even say such a thing.

So whether you are a historian, or a military historian, I am sure that the photographs and accounts will be a delight and a great addition to your library.

Thank you to Peter, again for your service, one of our last surviving multi-war hero's. It has been my honor to know you and sit with you and talk, and to have your first book in my position. We are forever in your debt.

Sincerely, Sgt (former) Timothy Wright MOS 84B

God Bless You. ---

Introduction

In my opinion, the camera is the most powerful weapon in war.

Peter Paul Ruplenas was born in "Southie" otherwise known as South Boston, Massachusetts on October 5th 1918, the same year that John F. Kennedy was born. It was also the same year that WWI ended and a few years later, he grew up during the great depression.

In 1940 he met Hazel Elena Rice on a blind date and 6 weeks later married her. They would have been married 71 years this year but The Good Lord took her away in 1986.

"Rupy" entered the U.S. Army in 1940 and kept signing re-enlistment papers every 3 years until 1970 when he retired.
During that amazing career he served our country with honors during WWII, Korea & Vietnam.

In WWII he took 2 weeks of Camera training school and was shipped off to England and was a member of the 486th (Heavy) Bomb Squadron. He conned his way onto 6 Bomb raids with the help of the Pilots before being caught by his Commander.
His days flying in a B-17 bomber were cut short, and that was a good thing as many of those planes did not make it back.

He also ran track and had a very impressive career with the Army but his proudest moment happened in Washington DC.
During his Honeymoon, in Washington DC, he took his wife Hazel to the Washington Monument. The elevator was getting crowded and he had Hazel get in, gave her his camera and said "I'll meet you at the top." The people in the elevator got a chuckle out of that thinking he would never make it. After all, the Monument is 555 feet tall. What the folks in the elevator did not know was that my father was in fantastic physical shape. They saw it minutes later as when the elevator opened, he was standing there to greet them with this smart aleck remark... "What took you so long?".

After WWII he went back to Southie and made Razor blades at Gillette and before you knew it, he re-enlisted. They shipped him off to Japan where a few years later his first son David was born in Sendai which took a huge hit with the recent Tsunami.

Two years later the Korean "conflict" broke out. To this day it has never officially been declared a War, shame. He was blown 20 feet in the air from a tank that exploded 50 feet in front of him and lost most of his hearing from constant artillery shelling all around him. He has permanent back damage from flying into a rock during a heavy battle in the rice paddies.

He suffers from frostbite, his toes are deformed and in constant pain, but thankfully made it home. He told me that sentry scouts were stationed in between mountain ranges and the weather hit 50+ below zero. In the morning he saw what that did to them; they did not make it through the brutal cold.

In Vietnam he was shot in the hand and has nerve damage. I can only imagine the horrible things he saw. You can see the horror through his photographs. I also think he changed as you can see in photos taken of him.

He worked covertly with "Rice's Raiders" a Guerrilla Hit and run tactical team that went behind enemy lines and decimated the enemy by destroying the weapons and incinerating any huts or houses that gave them shelter. He got a special medal for that.

When the 7th Infantry Division reached the Manchurian border, there was a great photo op. My Father was the 3rd American to reach the river. There is a famous photo of him photographing 2 soldiers there. The General posed for a photo and then spat in the water and said something to the effect "Screw the gooks" (so much for political correctness). He turned his back on about 1000 soldiers and tanks behind him and proceeded to urinate in the river. Who do you think followed him in relieving himself? Do I really have to spill those beans?

After the Korean War, he spent 10 years in Japan and the Far East photographing many generals, dignitaries and celebrities including Johnny Cash, Sugar Ray Robinson, Francis Albert Sinatra, Generals MacArthur, Bob Hope and many more. Those photos were made into a book and given to him as his 95th Birthday present.
That surprise party was in Brunswick Maryland during Railroad Days. A month later he was their Grand Marshall at their 81st Veterans Day parade!

When Vietnam came, he was shipped off to Hawaii and was with an Elite Crew called DASPO (Department of Army Special Photographers Organization). They spent time in Vietnam and then Hawaii; it was not always easy for him there. Or any soldier for that matter.

He retired in 1970 but before that he shot many photos for White Sands Missile Range, many which we will never see.

My Father just turned 95 and maybe he cannot run up the Monument anymore but if given the choice, he would reenlist and go back into the thick of things with his Speed-graphic camera. He thinks digital photography and photoshop are cheating. Maybe they are but for me it is less expensive.

Pops is survived by me, his granddaughter Elena, and thousands of amazing photos and stories. My wife Lorena cooks and cares for him, his 3 cats keep him warm at night and Bobi the dog entertains him.

I like to take him to Reunions, The Wall, Rolling Thunder and any other thing I can do where he can visit other Vets. This past year I crossed something off of MY Bucket list, he got to ride in the Rolling Thunder Parade. He also got to speak with R. Lee Ermey for nearly an hour before his handlers told him he had to go.

Pops is not a Marine but "Gunnery Sgt. Hartman" enjoyed his company. I want to thank him and ALL VETERANS of the United States of America for their service to the Greatest Country where Freedom is not free.

Thank You Pops!

John Ruplenas
PO Box 512
Gerrardstown WV 25420
2cameras3wars@gmail.com

ARTILLERY

The 7th Infantry Division

Artillery sends rounds over the mountaintop to alleviate North Korean firepower in their advance.

Soldiers take cover from enemy explosions

155mm Artillery Howitzer fires on the North Korean enemy ahead of advancing 7th Inf. Div troops.

Crew unload new supply of shells and arm them immediately for use.

A spotter watches hits on the mountain as my Division artillery clears the top for troops to climb against the enemy.

Artillery shelling clears forward hills before infantrymen advance.

Artillery shelling over a hill held by the enemy. We took this hill shortly after this.

Artillery shelling in the frigid snow getting ready to move up; trying to stay warm in the 32 degree below weather.

Artillery shelling standing by, awaiting orders to fire.

Spotter watches hits as artillery clears tops for troop climb.

A heavy mortar crew from the 17th RCT, 7th Infantry Division softens up the enemy two hills away from their position as infantrymen are ready to cross the river in boats.

Spotters saw that a concrete bunker on the enemy hill was directing their firepower on the advancing GIs and held up our drive.

It took this mortar, American tank and artillery fire before the North Koreans were finally driven out and deserted their concrete bunker and hill positions.

This action took place three miles north of Umyang-Ni in Korea.

9 April 1951

Mortars Coming In

Three well spread out GIs of "A" Company, 13th Eng. BN take cover behind rice paddy dike.

When they had saturated the area, they and advancing infantry pulled back.

They moved up later towards Yang-Gu.

Men of A Company, 13th Engineer BN, 7th Div. take cover from enemy mortars in a skirmish on the outskirts of Yanggu, Korea.

They were well spread apart to lessen any possible hits by the enemy.

15 April 51

MORTARS

A mortar crew with the 32nd RCT., 7th Infantry Division fires off another 4.2 round at the retreating North Korean and Chinese forces at the summit of the hill.

The enemy attacked the GIs at the top of the hill after dark the night before, and was still pulling back at daylight.

The Sgt. in charge of this crew said that four mortars fired approx. 1,700 rounds in the six hours and twenty-five minutes of the attack.

Barrels overheated and glowed in the dark. Firing was delayed until they cooled off. Some of the GIs used oiled rags to wipe and cool off the mortars.

This was the last round fired that morning as the enemy deserted the hill leaving many dead; also grenades, burp guns, rifles and gear.

GIs estimated that hundreds were killed, but most of the bodies were dragged back by the retreating enemy.

The Sgt. also told me that rounds he had left, as seen in the photograph, is all they had until a new supply that arrived by ship in Pusan would reach them 'in a few days.'

The action took place near the Hwachon Reservoir.

23 April 1951.

BRITISH COMMONWEALTH FORCES AT U.N.C.
HEADQUARTERS IN SEOUL, KOREA, CLEAN
THEIR FIELD PIECE IN DAILY WORK. 1962

Photo By: S/Sgt. Peter "Rudy" Ruplenas

10

An unidentified number of communist soldiers were in a house off the roadside as 7th Infantry Division was advancing along the road.

The GIs were getting sniped at. So instead of troops risking death, not knowing the number of enemy in the house or behind the stone walls, they called for mortar fire.

Smoke billows upwards as a mortar team of the 7th Inf. Div. makes a direct hit with a white phosphorous shell on the house N.E. of Chae Jae, Korea containing the communist soldiers. No more firing was heard after the "hit."

No GIs were hit by the first enemy fire.

12 March 1951

7th Inf. Div. fired artillery shells to clear out a Village in their advance through South Korea.

BRIDGES

All along this mountain road near Tehon-Ni, North Korean blew away sections of the pass.

Even infantrymen could not advance because the drop below varied from a few feet to hundreds.

The 13th combat engineer Battalion. Company "A" 7th Infantry Division is cross piecing more logs before finally filling road for traffic.

They had the bridge passable later on in the day for foot soldiers and heavy equipment to advance.

13th combat engineers

3 miles north of Ami-Dong Korea, 13th combat engineers 7th Infantry Division again repair a bridge with the center section completely blown away.

By the next day, the road span was repaired for foot & vehicle traffic.

This 7th Infantry Division unit always solved problems quickly and never was stumped in any engineering field problem.

This was 3 miles north of Ami-Dong.

2 March 1951

The retreating North Korean military destroyed all they could along the way. The UN troops by-passed them over roads and ditches in hot pursuit.

The 3rd platoon Company "D" 13th Combat Engineers showed their love to the Division's CG David Barr by naming the bridge for him after massive repairs made it safe for heavy vehicles to pass.

The Han River into Seoul, a steel and mobile Bridge (photo taken in heavy rain)

UN forces and Korean civilians watch US airstrikes on the enemy as they pull back from the UN Ground forces.

Close Ups

Al Chang

"To my pal and a real
  photographer, Rupy;
  one of the best during
  the Korean War.
Hope we can work
  together someday.
My best wishes and
Aloha from The
  Pineapple Kid, Al Chang."

Al Chang was one of the
greatest Military photographers of all time.
Chang was wounded three times as a military combat
photographer.
Like myself he covered WWII, Korea, and Vietnam.
Chang later worked for the Associated Press and was
twice nominated for a Pulitzer Prize.
He shot the classic image below during the Korean War
of a solider being comforted.

Cpl. Garmaker, 7th Infantry Division P.I.O. interviews a member of the 2nd Ranger Company, An All Black Unit after they came back from an assault. An enemy sniper forced the three of us back while taking this photo.

All Army basketball Game Seoul 1956

48th Battalion Phone A 48th Field Artillery Battalion. Officer and two enlisted men sit in the rain besides a bunker, waiting for firing orders over the phone.
The 48th is assigned to the 7th Inf. Div.

A GI Riding Roller Coaster in Japan with my friend Eva Duvall.

A warm fire, warm food and hot coffee helps relax tankers and Anti-Tank and Mine Platoon enlisted men of the 7th Infantry Division. The men took a well needed break before moving up to the front lines to support advancing infantry of the division.

The Communication Section of the 7th Infantry Division's 7th Signal Company had to provide all communications for the entire division twenty-four hours a day.
This was done during monsoons, heat waves, blizzards and temperatures that at one time reached 32° below zero.
A lineman pulls the wires taut as two polemen secure the same high up on the poles.
The lines were being installed near the town of Todon-ni in Korea.
The communication section earned a Meritorious Unit Commendation from the 8th Army for their Performance of Outstanding Service to the division from the Inchon landing on 16 Sept. 1950 until 16 March 1951.
Photo taken on 23 February 1951

Beating on a captured Chinese drum, this infantryman of the 7th Infantry Division seems to lack the musical talent of Gene Krupa.

If the facial reaction of his two buddies is any indication of critics, he had better give up any musical future.

Though all of them have been subjected to the sounds of heavy battle since they landed in Korea, they said his music was "the worst sound that they have ever heard in Korea."

The drum was among many articles left behind when the enemy retreated after a night-long battle on the divisions' front line of resistance.

After the overture, the combat medic returned to his outfit "for peace and quiet".

This did not last long and when I tried to get their names, incoming fire started to come in.

1951.

Captain Robert Flint and the 7th photo lab check motion picture film with GIs of our unit along with a Korean worker

For recreation some GIs went hunting and this one had a direct hit.

Soldiers relaxing in the Base Service Club playing pool before the start of the Korean War.

25

CPL Wilfred Hunkins,

7th Div Still Photographer

Cpl. Hunkins coming back from a patrol.   The rocky stream he is coming back from was the scene of a bloody battle.

Cpl. Hunkins photographing the troops returning fire on the front lines

Cpl Wilfred Hunkins, 7th Inf. Div still photographer, horses around with a mobile fire truck in a village where the division was advancing.

Cpl. Wilfred Hunkins put a Chinese POW tag on and waves two enemy weapons as he tries to be sent to a rear POW stockade to get a free ride home back to San Francisco. Having a sense of humor at times helped you during the War.

Cpl. Wilfred Hunkins (San Francisco) all loaded up for the convoy to continue forward.
The crowds of village children gather about "Hunk"

Cpl. Francis Wise (Wharton, OH) from Company "G" 32nd RCT relaxes and reads "fast, loose & lovely" while resting during a break.
His unit was advancing against Chinese Communist forces North of Pyongchang, Korea. His unit had very few days to relax.
24 Feb 1951

A young infantryman with the 32nd RCT, 7th Infantry Division enjoys his first wash in a month.
His unit was on the fighting front for over 30 days. When his unit was pulled into reserve for a few days, the nearest river became his bathtub.

Despite the coldness and ice in the river, he had a long and enjoyable footbath.
He had to jump out of the water right after I took this photo as an enemy sniper started to open up on him.
Feb 1951

GIs & Medics - battle weary troops. Medics of 7th Division take 40 winks at aid station shortly before one of our major pushes. The Medics and Infantrymen have been in continuous combat for days and needed this short respite from the front lines.

GIs, MEDICS and BAD FEET   While 13th Combat Engineers rebuild a blown mountain pass, men of Company C & F, 32nd RCT, 7th Infantry Division, rest on a roadside after taking an objective, at Hwaan, Korea. The 7th Medics check feet for trench foot, frostbite, or any other problems and treat them on the spot.   14 March 1951

INCHON COFFEE- Day Plus One at Inchon 7th Div
The GIs and officers have a short coffee break before
moving North after enemy soldiers that were
retreating.

MPs & ORPHAN - GIs check packages of fleeing
civilians for weapons or other banned articles at a
roadblock south of Seoul, Korea. This orphan was
found alone and adopted by the MPs. He was given a
uniform with rank, a safe home and meals.

Sept. 1950

MSG Fred MOSER, a combat photographer with the 7th Signal Company, 7th Infantry Division photo lab aligns his camera and mount before taking off in a spotter plane. Using a K-20 aerial camera, this mission is to photograph enemy buildup on mountain ridges ahead of the advancing division. Autographed photo inscribed "Good Luck You Lucky Bastard Fred Moser"
April 1951

PFC Peterson, a 7th Signal photographer leaves himself a big target as he photographs 7th Infantry Division firing on enemy ahead. They were members of 7th Reconnaissance at Yachon-Ni Korea. He was using his Rolleiflex then instead of an US Army Speedgraphic. 16 April 1951

Music soothes the relaxing GI", or so the "olde saying sayeth". At least PFC Robert F. McBeth, (Dennison, Oh) provides background music to his buddies as they take a letter writing and chow break near YULE-TONG. With this short "much needed" break in front line combat, PFC David KUNKEL (Evening Shade, Arkansas) finds time to drop his family in the states a few lines from the combat zone. McBeth found the gramophone and records during his units' advance and provided a little enjoyment for the combat weary troops. The men are with the 7th Infantry Division.   28 April 1951

On a short break UN forces check maps and radio messages from Army headquarters.

1951

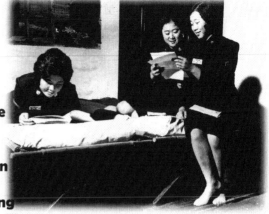

ROK WACs share a letter from home during off-duty hours in the barracks at the WAC Training Center in Seoul. The cots are placed on raised platforms but the girls do not have the luxury of a heated floor. In common with Korean custom, they remove their shoes before stepping onto the platform.

Technicians clean the mirror and proceed with a mechanical checkup of components of this searchlight. The searchlight unit moved into the 7th Infantry Division area to intensify night vision on the front lines where heavy enemy forces were dug in.
The searchlights diminished the chance of sneak enemy attacks on the dug-in Division infantry.

Romanowski Autographed "To Rupy Best of Luck Cpl. John Romanowski Korea 1950" Taking a breather from the endless combat that he has photographed, one of the top cinematographers of the Korean War relaxes against his jeep. From the North Korean invasion in June of 1950, the Pusan perimeter, the breakthrough and north across the 38th, he has used thousands of feet of film in his 35mm spider Eyemo camera documenting the war for the Dept. of Defense. CPL John ROMANOWSKI is assigned to the photo unit of GHQ in Tokyo and received his training at the army photo school at Ft. Monmouth in NJ. He was a classmate of mine. We met again in Korea when the break-through occurred and the unit he was covering linked up with the 7th Infantry Division. September 1950

Taxi - MOVE OVER MASH! PETE'S HACK COMPANY.
Cpl. Robert Peterson (Detroit, MI) assists Cpl. Wilfred
Hunkins (San Francisco, CA) from a Korean taxi that
they thought they could fix up. After looking it all over
they decided that it was "out" an engine, windows, seats,
etc. "Hunk" said it'd cost too much to repair, so they left
it. Both are top still photographers with the division
photo section.

Tired out infantrymen of the 7th Infantry Division try
to get a few minutes of sleep. No tents, no huts, just
Mother Earth.

TOM STONE

One of the top war correspondents to cover the Korean War was Tom Stone, Washington D.C. Award winner. Tom, with the Associated Press, does not need help to write his war communiqués to his main office. Tom scans the pages for the correct word in "A Dictionary of Slang and Unconventional English (Much like I speak)", a recently donated book to help him spice up his War stories. Tom has covered the 7th Infantry Division for many months and gets his stories up front with the infantry, where he is usually seen. The book was one of two found in a missionaries' abandoned house in the area. He was well liked by us, unlike some of the civilian press.   **14 March 1951**

WAC FEATURE STORY   SEOUL KOREA '63

GIs WINDOW WATCH - Two 7ᵗʰ Infantry Division GIs cover a suburban street near Seoul from shelled building being used as medical holding cell.
Sept. 1950

Bob Hope

16 March 1951

GIs WATCH SHOW

Any type of entertainment drew huge crowds to shows, be it Bob Hope or anyone in the theatre, movies or sports field. At this show, just a few miles from the front lines, GIs enjoy the music and comedy of Grandpa Jones and his group of entertainers.

Even lovers of big Bands and Jazz enjoy this brief respite from combat and, for today, joined the hundreds of lovers of country and western music.

Bob Hope brings laughter to battle weary 7th Infantry Division GIs from a swimming pool in Pusan. Some were lucky with the best seats in the house, the high tree limbs in back. These GIs were just a few miles from the North Korean troops.

GI horsing around

Signal Corps Photo Lab Headquarters

Soldier playing in sand

Seattle Washington - Leaving the States on the way to Korea 1955

South Korean President Park Chung-hee's son and his wife enjoy a sporting event in the Palace area of the capitol.

South Korean President's son

44

CASUALTIES

American GIs carry a dead body to a rear medical area for identification to ship him home.

Enemy dead and equipment litter the entire top and slopes of Hill 902, north of Ip-Tong in Korea where the "A" Company, 32nd RCT, 7th Infantry Division soldiers fought an all night battle against a massive North Korean attack.

The GIs had four 4.2 mortars as their only heavy firepower. The body in the photo is of a North Korean soldier. Besides this dead soldier, in the immediate area are smoke bombs, grenades, burp guns, ammo cans, rifles and supplies. The GIs held the line and stopped this soldier within feet of where they were dug in, right where the burp gun lay. The attack started at sunset and ended at sunrise.

23 April 1951

A soldier from Company" A", 32nd RCT, 7th Infantry
Division sweeps the hill among the dead North
Koreans looking for signs of any wounded enemy.
Just before midnight, the enemy attacked the
combat soldiers in a major attack that lasted until
sunrise. The well dug in Americans repelled charge
after charge.
The enemy bugles and drums echoed through the
mountain as every charge began.
With full night fading away, GIs could see hundreds
of enemy wounded and dead being dragged back
by their comrades.
At full daylight, GIs checking the hills like this one
found many dead and the entire face of the hill
littered with enemy equipment losses.
This rifleman passes enemy dead, grenades, rifles,
blankets and other equipment that are scattered all
over Hill 902 north of Ip- Tong.

                                        23 April 1951

A very badly
burned dead
civilian or
soldier off
the side of
the road.

Members of the 17th RCT, assigned to the 7th Infantry
Division repelled numerous enemy attacks all night long by
North Korean troops.
Some of the wounded and dead enemies were clad in U.S.
Army clothing and tried to fool the American defenders.
An infantryman, during the all night fight, brightly lit by a
full moon, said he almost let the dead soldier come over to
him. He noticed the army overcoat and the man spoke
some English. When he got closer he saw the man had
sneaker footwear plus "rank" shoulder boards.
The man got no further up the hill.
CPL. Joseph F. Cayse of Peoria, Illinois is pointing to the
buttons on the GI overcoat that was worn by this North
Korean officer. Cayse was with the unit that fought all
night long until the enemy withdrew at daybreak.
Action took place on a hill north of Kumma-Ri, Korea.
20 Feb. 1951

48

MASSACRE

While on a reconnaissance patrol with a 7th Infantry Division unit, the officer in charge was notified by villagers that the North Koreans had massacred villagers the day before.

We were told that villagers suspected of giving water, food or information to South Korean or other UN forces were taken out of their homes and bound with their hands behind them.

After the North Koreans left the area and fled north to avoid advancing 7th Infantry Division troops, they went looking for the villagers.

They found them, just as this photo shows hands still bound and the backs of their necks nearly severed by an ax or sword. There were four bodies in this ditch alone.

March 1951

D M Z

**While a North
Korean soldier
stands guard, a
North Korean
civilian
photographer
snaps a shot of
me.
Neither of us
passed our side
of the line.**

*Looking into No. Korea
61-62
from the DMZ*

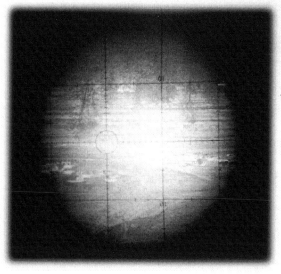

*Panmunjom Korea
Looking Through
8.0. Scope into
No. Korea 1962*

American and South Korean soldiers watch for enemy movements on DMZ line.

Who's fooling who? Look at the North Korean photographer trying to look inconspicuous as he is aiming his camera directly at me.

Two US Soldiers look in the window at the back of the meeting of the DMZ as a North Korean soldier looks directly at me. I was not intimidated.

The names "Armstrong and Glaser" are two of the GIs in our photo lab.

This is the truce talk area.

U.N. Staff waiting for N Korean delegates to arrive.

U.N. Truce Team looking though papers with North Korean delegates.

U.N. GROUP IN FOREGROUND ON DMZ LINES.

Debating between U.S. and N Korean staff. U.N. Staff on left.

Soldiers and civilian facing U.N. staff members at the start of meeting in DMZ line

**The DMZ or Military Demarcation Line;
UN staff and delegates more often than not
waited for the North Koreans to show up. They
were, like most women, fashionably late.**

A U.S.A. VISITING DIGNITARY
MEETS KOREAN TROOPS ON THE DMZ.
PHOTO BY S/SGT. PETER "RUPY"
RUPLENAS

HAL DRAKE, REPORTER WITH TOKYO STARS & STRIPED
INTERVIEWS A U.S. MILITARY MAN ON THE DMZ IN KORE
HE WAS DOING A STORY ON THE AMERICANS THAT PULLED
PATROL ON THE D.M.2.   KOREA 63

PHOTO BY: S/SGT. PETER "RUPY" RUPLENAS

Sort of like the Navy Seals (no disrespect to them), North Korean soldiers are peeking out through the bushes.

While the multinational delegates in the background watch, this North Korean soldier bumped into me 3 times when I was trying to take photos. The third time I bumped back into him so hard he started to draw his sidearm. The men behind me intervened and he left me alone after that. I guess I would never make a good diplomat.

UN Delegation talks at the DMZ Panjunmon Korea

U.S. MILITARY VISIT AND INSPECT A SOUTH KOREAN DEFENSE
POSITION ON THE D.M.Z. IN KOREA. ONE OF THE CIVILIAN
DIGNITARES EYES ENEMY POSITION, NOT TOO MANY YARDS ACROSS
THE LINE, THROUGH A HIGH POWERED SCOPE.
KOREA 1963
PHOTO BY: S/SGT. PETER "RUPY" RUPLENAS

While the North Korean soldiers watch, UN guards take their positions in Panjunmon at a meeting.

On the DMZ line that divides North and South Korea; I am awaiting the South Korean VIPs to arrive to start the meetings with the North.

**UN JOT (Joint Observers Team) awaits
North Korean to start another meeting.**

More often than not, they were late.

North Korean troops march by as they get ready for the UN Delegates meeting

In the Truce Talk area of DMZ

Field meeting on DMZ; both American and N Korean staff members reach for falling Document (Allies on left).

N.K. KOREANS IN WHITE SHIRTS

GENERALS

General MacArthur leaving Murphy Army hospital Waltham Mass after visiting casualties of war

Corps Commanders question a 7th Division, 32nd regiment driver.

All tanker of 7th Inf Div have every tool they use laid out on tarps for inspection by General from Army HDS.

SEOUL, KOREA, October 30, 1962 (United Nations Command) — — Maj. Gen. Van H. Bond, Acting Chief of Staff, United Nations Command, and Chief, Joint Military Assistance Advisory Group, Korea (ProvMAAG–K) leads a group of US and Korean dignitaries aboard the USS Queenfish at Chinhae Naval Base. The party remained aboard while the submarine conducted anti-submarine warfare exercises with elements of the ROK Navy. (OFFICIAL US ARMY PHOTO) BY:

S/SGT. PETER "RUPY" RUPLENAS

A full line of US Generals and British Big Brass "Stand In Line" for the National Anthems at Headquarters of the Army in Seoul.

American & South Korean Civilian Brass Stand - Seoul Korea. They are standing at attention as both national anthems are played.

Top Generals and Officers stand tall after a meeting before leading men into combat action.

The Big Brass, both American and Korean, stand tall during a ceremony outside Seoul.

Big Brass Salutes Color guard
UN Command Headquarters Knight Field, Seoul

Covering a parade with Generals marching by at UN Headquarters, Seoul Korea

GEN. GUY MELOY,
C.G. OF ALL U.N. TROOPS
IN KOREA, SALUTES
U.N. TROOPS IN SEOUL
DURING A FORMAL PARADE
1962

**Gen Guy Meloy
1962
UN Headquarters**

**He was the
"overall" boss of
all army troops**

**Gen Huston, Rupy, Col Newsome, Col Uree - 1952
Plaque Dedication at Wall of Headquarters in Seoul.
After covering the ceremonies, they asked me to
pose with them — quite an honor.**

**Gen. Walton Walkers visits Japan before Korean
War. He visited many units, conducting meetings
with commanding officers to make sure they were
combat ready.**

15AAA NORNMEGI Secretary Of The Army Pace
Sec. of the army Frank Pace has conference with U.S. Army Big Brass after leaving briefing with 7th Div. CG Maj. Gen. David Barr near the front lines.   Pace is on right wearing soft cap.

General Barr and Company
Col. Powell, 17th INF C.O. and Brigadier General Kiefer, C.G. of the 7th Infantry Division are briefed by C.O. 7th Infantry Division David Barr on situation in the southern area of South Korea.

General Barr assuring that each tanker has all the
equipment it needs for the 7th Inf. Div. tank units. If
they do not have all the tools, even the smallest one,
they did not move out with their buddy transfers
until they were 100% equipped.

**The sign says
"General Barr Bridge
Built by the 3rd
Platoon Company
"D" 13 Engineers
"Cross With Comfort"**

General Barr visiting 7th Inf. Div tank units to ensure that the tankers had all their necessary "Bill of Fare" before being permitted to join the front lines

General Barr inspection just short of the front lines
Missing one tool - stay in rear until fully equipped

General Bond aboard a South Korean submarine during peace time Korea. Right after I snapped this "Dive Dive" was announced and we went very deep. You could hear the propellors of sub chasers overhead but they never got to us.

Lt. General Ned Almond prepares to take off after a visit to 7th Inf. Division front lines. He is checking GI lines by air after takeoff.

Cpl. Hollis Miller stands by (on right) ready to photograph Gen. Douglas MacArthur as he leaves his headquarters in Tokyo Japan. He was a top still photographer. Hollis was a classmate of mine in photo school at Ft. Monmouth, a WWII combats infantryman, and was killed going into Korea when his plane loaded with photographers and journalists crashed. Hollis was on the Tokyo GHQ staff.   Spring 1950

Japanese and U.S. civilians await General MacArthur at his Headquarters in Tokyo Japan.

**General MacArthur addresses guests as he turns
Government of South Korea back to President Rhee.
Ceremonies were held in Capitol Building, Seoul, Korea.**
                                                    Sept 1950

**General MacArthur, at Murphy Army Hospital in
Waltham, Massachusetts visiting disabled War Vets with
the Hospital C.O.**

General MacArthur photo from Stars & Stripes

32. Left to right, Major General Doyle O. Hickey, Deputy Chief of Staff, GHQ; Syngman Rhee, President of the Republic of Korea; General of the Army Douglas MacArthur, Commander in Chief, UN Command; Mr. John Muccio, United States Ambassador to Korea; Vice Admiral Arthur D. Struble, and Major General Edward M. Almond confer in the Capitol building, Seoul, after ceremonies restoring the capital of Korea to its president, September 29, 1950. *U.S. Army photograph.*

General Mathew B. Ridgeway and Col. Powell leave their jeep to walk in and check the situation of our division that was dug in on the front lines.

Lt. Col. John H Chiles (Independence, Mo.), CO 23rd PCT, 2nd Div, on the 7th Divisions left flank, briefs Lt. Gen. Matthew B Ridgway, CG, Eusak, on enemy strong points now under attack. In rear (L to R) are major Joseph W Dale (New Orleans, LA), aide to Gen. Ridgway; major General Claude Farenbaugh, CG, 7th Infantry Division; Brig Gen. Homer Kiefer, CG, 7th Div. Army

General Walker tells troops about battle affairs and what they will be facing.

(L to R) SFC Ervin G. Tweed (Ft. Benning, GA), M/Sgt. Thomas Mulholland (Birmingham, AL), both with HD . 17th RCT reminisce with Lt. Gen. Matthew B. Ridgeway, CG Eusak, at a Regimental CP north of Pyongchang, close to the front lines.   Sgt. Tweed knows the General from boyhood while Sgt. Mulholland served with Gen. Ridgeway in the 82nd Airborne division.

Generals Seoul Korea Conference

Korea Honors Gen. Le May

Photo by "Rupy"

Air Force Chief of Staff General Curtis E. LeMay receives the Republic of Korea Order of Service Merit, First Class, in Seoul from General Chung Hee Park, acting ROK president, while an unidentified man helps with the presentation. LeMay was in Korea Thursday and Friday to inspect U.S. and ROK military facilities. (U.S. Army photo SFC Peter P. Ruplenas)

Major General Claude B. Fenerbaugh receives information from a 32nd Infantry officer on the situation.

Major General Claude B. Ferenbaugh observing artillery fire. The general spots the hits on the hills ahead made by our division. The officer beside him briefs him about the targets.   1951

8th Army General congratulates MSG Track Events Seoul Korea

A US General and his staff check soldiers as to their equipment and attitude before the Sergeant heads to the Combat Zone.

Albert Provost from the Radio Section, Maj Gen McGraw, Lt. Col Bill Buerkle, Brig Gen Pattison

Big Brass of US Military stand tall at a formal ceremony in Korea.

**American
Generals
Social Affair
S. Korea**

Brig. Gen. Kiefer (CG 7th Inf.,) Maj. Gen. Ferenbaugh (CG 7th Div.) & Brig Gen. Sink (Asst. CO 7th Div.) celebrates Ferenbaugh's 52nd Birthday in a combat zone.
The nickname of the division was "Hour Glass" but later it was changed to "Bayonet", thus the Birthday cake included a bayonet in the cake

One WAC salutes, the other takes pictures as Gen. MacArthur and an aide leave headquarters in Tokyo for lunch.

Spring 1950

**Gen. Lenmitzer
Inspects 7th Inf. Div.
Korea**

**General checking out our bedding
Of course we did not have good bedding out in the
open cold mountain ranges.**

General Curtis
"Iron Pants"
Lemay

General
Guy Meloy
Front Lines
DMZ Korea

General Kiefer

Lt. General J. Lawton Collins visits 7th Infantry Division troops in field in Honshu Japan shortly before start of Korean War in 1950. Lt. General Walton H (Bulldog) Walker smiles as General Collins talks to a 7th Div. LT, who I think was General Walkers' son. A 9th Corps CO stands by.

General Palmer and a top 8th Army brass enter the 8th Army top head - quarters in Seoul Korea

General Myers Seoul Korea 1963

US Army General Hays checks out troops on a visit.

United Nations Officers Club Seoul Korea 1962

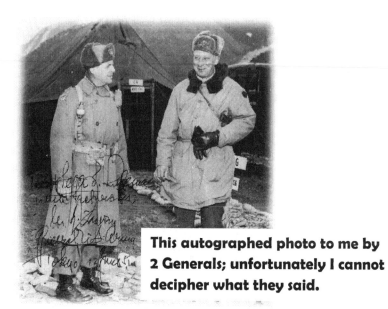

This autographed photo to me by 2 Generals; unfortunately I cannot decipher what they said.

Lt. General Samuel Myers 7th Infantry Division displays at an Army Hospital headquarters in Seoul Korea

GEN. GUY MELOY, C.G. OF
ALL TROOPS IN SOUTH KOREA &
DIGNITARY LOOK AT OIL PAINTING
OF GEN. HODES ON ARMY HD. WALL.
DEDICATION WAS IN RESPECT OF
GEN. HODES WHO DIED RECENTLY
HD. QTRS BUILING WAS
RENAMED "HODES" HALL
IN MEMORY OF GEN. HODES
ON 12 NOV. 1962

**General Guy S. Meloy UN Command, Seoul Korea
Korean Interpreter**

Parade
 Knight Field
 UNC HD
 Seoul Korea

Honor Guard
Kimpo Air Base
Seoul Korea

US Army, Navy and Military White House Team Visit Korean Front Line 1963

PRESIDENT PARK CHUNG HEE   SEOUL, KOREA 1961

I took photos of U.S. Army "Big Brass Guest" on the president's grounds - President stopped and shook my hand. WOW

South Korean President Park Chung-hee

He was assassinated in 1979 during a dinner at a Korean Central Intelligence Agency (KCIA) safe house inside the Blue House presidential compound, Gungjeong-dong, Seoul by Kim Jae-kyu, who was the director of KCIA and the president's security chief.
Four bodyguards and a presidential chauffeur were also killed.

99

South Korean President Park Chung-hee cont.

It is known as "10.26" or the "10.26 incident" in South Korea.
By the time of his assassination, President Park had exercised dictatorial power over South Korea for nearly 18 years.
The Korean Central Intelligence Agency was created in 1961 to coordinate both international and domestic intelligence activities, including those of the military.

Almost immediately following its creation, the KCIA was used to suppress any domestic opposition to Park's regime; using its broad powers to wiretap, arrest, and torture anyone without a court order.
KCIA was heavily involved in many behind-the-scene political maneuverings aimed at weakening the opposition parties through bribing, blackmailing, threatening, or arresting opposition lawmakers.
President Park nevertheless nearly lost the presidential election to Kim Dae-jung in 1971 despite spending ten percent of the national budget on his election campaign.
Park therefore established the Yushin Constitution in 1972 to ensure his perpetual dictatorship.
This abolished the direct vote in presidential elections and replaced it with an indirect voting system involving delegates, allotted one third of the National Assembly seats to the president, gave the president the authority to issue emergency decrees and suspend the Constitution, gave the President the authority to appoint all judges and dismiss the National Assembly, and repealed a term limit to presidency. (Source: Wikipedia)

JAPAN

Being taught how to use chopsticks while I was stationed in the Orient with the 7th Division

Dominos or Pizza Hut has nothing on this delivery man! Loaded with trays of food, he heads out to deliver on his route.

Sightseeing in Tokyo Japan

Migatske near the Main Gate of Camp Schimm Sendai Japan 1955. My first born son David was born in Sendai.

Sightseeing Tokyo Japan on my day off wearing civilian clothes

Standing across US Military High Headquarters Tokyo Japan

**GI
riding
roller
coaster in
Japan**

**Children's Playground on rooftop of Matsuza department
store on the Ginza   Tokyo, Japan 1957**

**Iamachi Japan
1949 –
Christmas Day
Earthquake**

1949 Iamachi Christmas Day Earthquake

JEEPS, PLANES
and other VEHICLES

Half Track 4-50 Cal Guns "Hot Stuff No. 2" awaits further orders to engage the enemy.

½ TRACK TRACKS
While an infantrymen and I hit the ditch due to heavy incoming small arms fire, a division halftrack from 7th Recon, named Frances, returns incoming fire with three guns.   In the ditch I was safe from incoming fire.

The 7th Infantry Division GIs stand by for orders with their mechanized vehicle on the banks of the Han River. They are checking their results on the enemy ahead so GI's can cross safely. Smoke on other side of embankment is from 7th Division Artillery Firepower.   Sept 1950

8th Army moves safely along mountain roads as they head for the retreating North Korean enemy.

Enlisted men of Battery "D", 15th AAA Field Artillery Battalion open fire with their quad 50 caliber machine guns at enemy held positions on hill 860. Advancing infantrymen of the 17th RCT, 7th Infantry Division received heavy

enemy fire, and called for heavy firepower support. The assault continued against communist forces dug in north of KAOCH'ANG-NI, Korea. Some of the infantrymen named the quad 50s 'Chicago Pianos', like the guns used during the 20-30s gang wars.

An unidentified Lt. of the 32nd Inf. Regiment, 7th inf. Div. fires a 30 Caliber machine gun at an enemy hillside at Ami-Dong, Korea. The firing became very heavy and we both had to pull back after being fired upon while moving up ahead of advancing combat soldiers.   1 March 51

96th FA with the 7th Div. Inf moves up as a Jeep is disabled in the river.

A soldier has time to relax in a jeep before moving up to the combat lines.

USE THIS CAPTION

MAJ. ANGUS J. WALKER, DIRECTOR, PHOTOGRAPHY DIVISION, GHQ, FAR EAST COMMAND POSES BY A AMERICAN T-6 PLANE NEAR TAEGU, KOREA IN 1950. HE WAS ABOUT TO TAKE OFF ON A PHOTO RECON MISSION NEAR THE FRONT LINES.

AFTER RETIRING FROM THE ARMY, HE HELD VARIOUS POSITIONS IN THE BOSTON AREA. AT THE AGE OF 77 HE WAS ORDAINED A PRIEST IN THE MISSIONARY SOCIETY OF THE HOLY APOSTLES.

BEST COMBAT PHOTO — An unidentified lieutenant of the 32nd Infantry Regiment fires a 30 caliber machine gun at the enemy. Sgt. Rupena says the haze, smoke, wreckage and mutilated trees which depict war so well make this his best combat photo of the war. The picture was taken in March, 1951, near Ami-Dong, Korea, with four by five Graphic.

One of our jeeps driving up front was fired upon by the enemy. He had to drive off the road and was sprayed by incoming fire. This was selected as the "BEST COMBAT PHOTO"

A 7th Division unit going out on a Recon Patrol gives a few infantrymen a taxi ride!

BUGGING OUT!

Convoy of vehicles and troops of the 17th Rct. withdraw to new defense lines under brutal enemy fire. They set up new positions south of Anyang-Ni. There were no losses to our troops.

Destruction of various US Army War equipment lies along sandy areas of Korea.

TRACK MOVING UP

More division track vehicles move up to support 7th Infantry Division in hills up ahead. The roads ahead were safe.

A Division truckload of GIs moves up with supplies in the trailer.
They made sure to roll up many straw mats for comfort at their next sleep-over.
The 7th Division engineers provided taxi service all throughout the war.

HIT THE DIRT!

Men of 13th Combat Engineers were heading off to repair a blown up bridge in Ami-Dong, Korea when an enemy burp gun saturated the area. They all "bailed out" of the dump truck with no casualties. A division tank moved up and cleared the area. The GI on right still has not hit the deck. They moved up shortly with no resistance.

March 1951

GI FIRES FROM JEEP

PFC Talmadge L. Turner (Newberry SC.) with 32nd RCT, 7th Infantry Division returns enemy burp gun fire coming from hillside near Ami-Dong. He and fellow GIs were bringing supplies and ammo up to advancing troops. They moved towards the North Korean line shortly thereafter due to PFC Turner and other American firepower.   **1 March 1951**

RUNNING FOR COVER

Men of the 17th RCT, 7th Infantry Division run for cover further down the road when enemy mortars started to drop all around them ½ mile south of Yangcu Korea. GIs beat a hasty retreat as the North Koreans 'walk in' heavy mortars on the advancing 7th Division, 17th RCT units.   After finding concealed positions of the enemy spotters, artillery from the divisions' heavy guns knocked out the enemy positions and the GIs advanced a few minutes later.   YANGGU Korea   15April 1951

Trucks, jeeps and other vehicles move up; getting ready to cross the Han River.

HELL ON WHEELS

A unit of the 32RCT was scheduled to attack dug in enemy on the hills north of CHAE-JAE. Prior to their advance, a half-track from the units 15 AAA strafes the hillsides with their 50 cal guns. The track named Hell on Wheels by the crew said the nickname was Chicago Piano. The spotter with binoculars checks results of the 7th Infantry Division firepower.　　13 March 1951

A 7th Infantry Division Jeep Convoy moves ahead of a "no fire" day meaning there was no enemy resistance.

A convoy of the 7th Infantry Division push northward through ruins of Kapsan, Korea. This motorized convoy of the 49th Field Artillery, 7th Infantry Division moves northward through the ruins of the city of Kapsan in North Korea. The city was destroyed by Allied air and ground artillery as the 17th RCT advances towards the town of Hyesanjin, on the Yalu River. The 49th provided artillery support for the advance in sub-zero weather, but enemy resistance at this point was very light. 20 Nov 1950

One of the few days we got a "taxi" ride to cross a really cold river. This helped 7th Infantry Division photographers take pictures of action on dry land.

A Quad 50 Cal machine gun is fired by men of the 15th AAA, 7th Inf. Div. at enemy troops north of Norumegi Korea in support of advancing troops of the 17th RCT, 7th US Inf. Div. **7 Apr 51**

PFC John Cook (Syracuse, NY) 7th Reconnaissance Battalion, 7th Infantry Division runs towards a 7th Reconnaissance 30 cal machine gun loaded down with belts and cans of ammunition under sniper fire across rice paddies at Yachon-Ni, Korea.

Members of a 7th Infantry Division unit were running out of ammo when a half-track pulled up on the road leading to the village.

The track gunner opened up with his 50-caliber machine gun, as an infantryman takes cover from the sniper fire at the back of the track.

After a couple of strafing passes by a U.S. Air Force jet on the enemy hillside just a few hundred yards ahead, fresh infantry moving up secured the village later in the day.

All the enemy deserted the village of Yachon-Ni when the 17th RCT troops advanced.

16 April 1951

A mechanized vehicle moves along Korean roads

UN convoy moves up with equipment and men towards the retreating North Korean forces.

US Army Supply depot containing trucks, jeeps and other vehicles line up for supplies

USAF Jet drops bombs on enemy targets ahead of advancing American troops.

7th Inf Div Han River Mechanized Vehicle

Assorted Photos of Jeeps and Mechanized vehicles

A convoy of the 7th Infantry Division push northward through ruins of Kapsan, Korea.

This motorized convoy of the 49th Field Artillery, 7th Infantry Division, moves northward through the ruins of the city of Kapsan in North Korea.

The city was destroyed by Allied air and ground artillery as the 17th RCT advances towards the town of Hyesanjin on the Yalu River.

The 49th provided artillery support in the advance in sub-zero weather, but enemy resistance at this point was very light.

20 Nov 1950

My wife Hazel, with the cane, waits for us to fix a flat tire on a jeep on the 38th Parallel.

USAF

Tanks, Planes & Men on field near DMZ

Paratrooper Air Drop

KOREAN PEOPLE

A Korean worker takes a very large and heavy load of supplies to a customer in a peaceful town not affected by the War.

Korean Villagers forage for food after the enemy destroyed their village.

This Korean Soldier on horseback in full stride nails a bullseye!

A South Korean civilian, that did odd jobs for the 7th Infantry that were in a village for a few days, enjoys what he didn't have for days, a large bone loaded with meat thanks to the Unit's mess hall. We loved this man!

Children in

native outfits

getting ready

to dance in

a parade

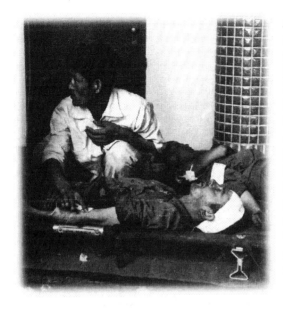

A South Korean civilian comforts a wounded 7th Infantry Division GI while they wait for medical help. Civilian medics used bombed out building to give first aid until able to drive them to medical aid stations. Civilians helped us a lot in medical situations. Seoul, Korea.

Sept 1950

A South Korean civilian comforts a wounded 7th Infantry Division GI while they wait for medical help.
Civilian medics used bombed out building to give first aid until 7th Division or US Marine Medics came to drive them to medical aid stations. There were many GIs treated by villagers to help us advance. We are so grateful for their help. Seoul, Korea.   Sept 1950

During the invasion of Seoul Korea, civilian nurses and doctors volunteered medical attention to American GIs of the 7th Div. and Korean nationals that were wounded by retreating North Korean soldiers. This was taken in a public building on the outskirts of Seoul.

ROK & WOUNDED GI

South Korean soldiers mill around as one of their medics gestures to civilians to bring one of their wounded into a house for treatment. The South Koreans were assigned to the 7th Infantry Division. Seoul, Korea.   Sept 1950

CIVILIAN GIVING INFORMATION
A 7th Infantry Division officer questions a civilian in outskirts of Seoul, Korea. He was given information on sections of city where North Korean were setting up ambushes. Our unit was advancing toward the capital.
Sept. 1950

Many troops were surprised by the work ethic of the Korean people. This young Boy near Cho-Gi Suwon carries a very heavy load on a country road.

Native dancing

Korean children playing near Suwon - no longer afraid of the US Army.

A KOREAN OLD "MAMA SAN" SWEEPS THE
49 STEPS, BETWEEN HER & A FRIENDS HOME.
SHE DOES THIS DAILY.   1962

PHOTO BY: S/SGT. PETER "RUPY" RUPLENAS

Korean

Parade

Cpl. Hunkins stops at a village to chat with some men keeping warm by a fire. Their village was not damaged at all by the enemy. They were very fortunate.

Native dressed woman in Seoul Korea 1957

**Papason
Seoul
Korea 1957**

Two men from a village

South Korean ladies with parasols take a walk on a road

Two Koreans dressed in native costume on top of a mountain

The 1000 steps Seoul Korea 1957
Completed in 1398, it was destroyed by an arsonist in
2008.   It was the Republic of Korea's #1 national
treasure.

A
Korean
flower
vendor

A country
farmer and
their property
unaffected by
the War

Downtown shopping in Seoul Korea 1963

An elderly Korean woman works in a field near her home.

Civilians enjoy walking and shopping through their cities that were rebuilt after the War.

Men of "A" Company, 17th RCT, 7th Infantry Division, pass through the ruined village of Yachon-Ni, Korea, as they pursue fleeing Chinese troops. 19 Apr 1951

Korean women carrying a very heavy load on her head

Koreans making sand bags

Watching a baseball game in Seoul Korea

Entering this city the banner says "Welcome UN Army"

The sign in this village thanking us for all the War effort and all the help they got afterwards says "WELCOME UN ARMY".

Villagers young and old alike stand by a country road to watch US Military convoy go by.

United States Army and Korean civilians are in a safe place during peace time.

**Very few water pipes were built so soon after the war.
Many of the Korean people carried buckets of water to their houses.
These folks are pumping for Water.
Seoul Korea 1957**

Koreans search for anything they can use after their village is devastated by the enemy.

My friend PFC William Dowlen is waiting for a bus Seoul Korea June 1957

Native Girl Korean Costume in Seoul Korea 1963

153

MINESWEEPER

The 7th Inf. Div. engineers and other units in the UN. When they could, they put up these signs in mined areas to prevent troops from walking on them.

MINES
DANGER

Enlisted men of the 7th Infantry Division FA Battalion probe for land mines in a field north of LLMANY ANG-NI, Korea. They were making sure the area was cleared of mines or booby traps before driving their field pieces into the field and setting up for fire support of the infantrymen. Some other fields had been mined, so orders were - check it out! Thank God there were no mines found here.   8 April 1951

Probing Mines

An engineer from the 13th Combat Engineer Battalion, 7th Infantry Division sweeps a section of the road where a division jeep was blown up by a mine.

The driver tried to "U-turn" the jeep and ran over the mine, buried in the shoulder of the narrow road. He was a war casualty.

Other engineers are ahead after sweeping this area, but one was missed in one of the heaviest mined roads that the division traveled on in the war. The enemy was far ahead so arms were not in the firing position.

13th BN Combat Engineers and 32nd RCT Infantrymen probe off the road for more mines after one of their tanks, "June", hit a mine throwing out the left track.

Fortunately no physical injuries to the tankers of 7th Inf. Div. and the infantry continued their forward drive.

MOVE OUT

The 32ⁿᵈ Infantry advances north of Pyong-Chong in good weather and no enemy fire for a change.

7th Inf safely advance Koach-Ang-Ri near Hill 680 with no enemy in sight.

7th Div. moves up far behind North Korean lines.

As they advance towards the Yalu River and the Manchurian border. This day the temperature was logged in at 20° below zero.   21 Nov. 1950

The well equipped 7th Inf. Div. advances on road with no incoming fire.

The 7th Inf. Div advances across a frigid river with no incoming enemy fire at the time.

17th RCT GIs climb a mountain near Sogu-Ri. They were not challenged by the enemy and we took this hill easy.

The 32nd RCT moving up towards An-Yang-Ni. They are with the 7th Inf. Div and close in line as spotters said the road is safe from the enemy.   19 Sept. 50

A 7TH Division Company 32nd RCT advances by a country lake in South Korea towards fleeing enemy. They are well spread out against possible enemy sniper fire. **Spring 1950**

ADVANCE TO FRONT:

Personnel of the 3rd Regiment, V & ROK, advance towards the front south of Hadaewa in the direction of Ami-Dong, Korea. They are there to assist the U.S. Army 7th Inf. Div. in driving the North Koreans out of the town. They are close up as a spotter plane said "No enemy ahead!"
1 March 1951

Advance elements of the 17th RCT, 7th Infantry
Division continues their drive towards the Yalu River
and the Manchurian border. Only a couple of
mortars were incoming, with no damage; plus a few
rounds of small arms fire every now and then.
The North Koreans were not the enemy this day,
Mother Nature was. Severe winds and sub-zero
temperatures coming down from Manchuria created
medical casualties.
Here, near the town of Sogu-Ri in North Korea, the
temperature was hitting the thermometers at 22°
BELOW zero. Most of the troops were not clad in
lined parkas, fleece lined boots, and other sub zero
gear.   Hundreds of potbelly stoves and winter
clothing were air dropped by the U.S. Air force to 7th
Inf. Division soldiers about a week later.
They had fought their way from the Iwon Landing
about 200 miles south and some in the Chosen
Reservoir, not clad for the sub zero days and nights.

16 Nov. 1950

Chinese communist attack as we bug out.

Members of Co. F and G, 17th RCT, 7th US Inf. Div. advance unopposed to Norumfgi Korea, two miles south of the 38th parallel.

7 Apr 51

Enemy gone? Our Division is still chasing them through a farm.

Members of Co F & G, 17th RCT, 7th Infantry Division, with tank support, advance unopposed to Morumegi, Korea, within two miles of the 38th Parallel. Unit is well spread out to minimize casualty count.

7 April 1951

UPHILL- GI's of E Company, 17th RCT, 7th Div climb Hill 675 North of Kumma-Ri Korea after crossing snow covered valley in the background. No enemy incoming fire at the time for our tired infantry.

24 Feb 51

GIs move on towards the North Koreans who were "bugging out", before checking out houses for the enemy.

A foot patrol from "H" Company, 17th RCT, 7th Infantry Division moves forward on a muddy road, during a heavy rain. They are on their way to support members of their unit a few miles north that came under heavy enemy fire earlier in the day.

They are a couple of miles south of YACHON-NI, Korea. The entire unit had to pull back later in the afternoon due to zero weather conditions that stopped all UN air and artillery support.

Infantrymen and supporting troops of Company "A" 17th RCT, 7th Infantry Division move up toward their objective, enemy held hill #860, and encounter retreating North Korean forces just northeast of Kaoch' Ang-Ni, Korea.

16 April 1951

Men of I Company, 32nd RCT, US 7th Infantry Division, advance north of Samgbanjong during their drive to outflank the city of Hadaewa, Korea. Enemy troops pulled back under 7th Infantry Division artillery fire.

Men of K Company, 32nd RCT, US 7th Infantry Division move into position along a dry riverbed just outside of the city of Hadaewa, Korea; preparing to launch an attack on the town.

28 Feb. 1951

HELP NEEDED—Medical aids of Company A, 32d RCT, 7th Infantry Division, hurriedly climb a hill in Korea for the fourth time during the day to carry aid to wounded American GIs. (**U.S. Army Photo by Sgt. Peter R. Ruplenas**)

The 17th RCT unit continued advancing towards Oron-Ni. The enemy held positions on the hills ahead. 7th Infantry Division had no contact with North Korean troops on Hill 887.

5 April 1951

Men of K Company, 32nd RCT, US 7th Infantry Division, pass grass and trees set afire by white phosphorous shell bombardment and trudge up the last few yards to the top of their objective, Hill 671 N.E. of Chae-Jae, Korea. They had support of ROK soldiers assigned to the unit. The enemy had retreated.

12 Mar 1951

Heavy-laden troops, carrying everything but footlockers on their backs, slosh their way up precarious hills. Snow and then heavy rains a few days before turned the hill into a slippery mud pile. The target of "K" Company, 32nd RCT, 7th Infantry Division was enemy held Hill 671, north of CHAE-JAE, Korea. 12 March 1951

Continuing the advance - winding along a Korean country road, infantrymen of Co. "A", 17th RCT, 7th Inf. Div. near the village of Kaoch Ang-Ni Korea as they continue advance against the Communist forces in that area. Like any smart GI, they marched far apart from each other.   24 Apr 51

Committing a big error, the GI has his mess kit hung on his pack instead of inside. Walking up the hill the mess kit catches the sun. Flashes could alert the enemy on other hillsides. His fellow troops chewed him out for this.

Our troops are awaiting orders to take the mountains the enemy held the day before.

This 7th Inf. Div. Patrol is well spread out to lessen any incoming enemy fire as they go on a reconnaissance patrol in this bleak terrain.

As division armored vehicles dig in, a small Recon
Patrol moves out to scan the area ahead for enemy
activities. I was 2nd right, behind Officer Leading
Patrol. I was a Cinematographer. John Romanski,
with camera, follows lead man to shoot any action.
Photo by Daniel Thompkins   Sept 1950

A 7th Inf. Div. unit has orders to move out and break
down their tent city.

GIs of "E" Company, 17th RCT, 7th Infantry Division "haul ass" as heavy rifle and machine gun fire saturates the area that they were in. A river crossing was delayed until tank and rifle fire silenced the incoming fire that the North Koreans were throwing at them. They later took the hill after the river crossing and after a bunker with three foot walls built by the communists was destroyed. This action took place near Umyang-Ni in Korea.

9 April 1951

Well spread out soldiers move up roads and rice paddies after retreating from the enemy.

A unit of the 17th RCT, 7th Infantry Division cross muddy rice paddies and streams near Yumok'Tong in Korea. Despite the steady rain and sloppy walking conditions, the unit continues to advance against positions held by Chinese Communist Forces in the area. Division artillery could not be used due to the low visibility on the hills.

19 April 1951

Walking through trenches dug by enemy troops, infantrymen of Co "A" 17th RCT, 7th Infantry Division advance towards their objective, Hill #860, as UN troops continue their assault against the communist forces near Kaoch And-Ni, Korea. There was no incoming enemy fire.   **24 Apr 1951**

177

The 17th RCT continues its pullback from the front
lines as weather continues to hamper visual contact
with the communist enemy. Airstrikes and artillery
and mortar fire ceased as the forward observers
could not see the results of the strikes.

The rain and fog completely covered most of the
enemy held hills so higher headquarters back
ordered the pull. The action took place in the
YUMOK'TONG area.

19 April 1951

POW

POW - A North Korean Officer (with boots) sits with some of his captured men as a South Korean soldier guards them; prior to moving them to a stockade. This was in the 7th Inf. Div. troops area of operations on outskirts of Seoul, Korea.   **Sept 1950**

2 captured North Korean soldiers

A medic from the 7th medical company has captured
Chinese POW unwrap his filthy bindings on his severely
frost bitten feet. He was sent back to a POW Stockade in
the rear. When they had time, our medics treated anyone
that needed help, including North Korean troops and
civilians.

American soldiers are checking civilian clad Koreans
as suspected North Korean personnel. One was
detained, the others let go.

Capture of POW in Storm

A rifleman of the 32nd RCT fires at the enemy at the base of the hill, as the Tank Gunner prepares to assist. The North Korean prisoner is awaiting a jeep to take him to G2. He was wearing a North Korean Officers Uniform under his civilian clothing. Action was north of Ami-Dong.
6 March 1951

ROK & American Soldiers of the 32nd RCT 7th Inf. Division march Chinese Communist POW's captured by members of advance units of the 32nd RCT to POW camp North of Pyonchang Korea.

Capture of POW in Storm

Severe snowstorms held up the infantry advances of
many army units in the Korean War. The infantry troops
were dug in a mile or so in back of this listening post.
The 32nd RCT, 7th Infantry Division sent a tank and a few
infantrymen about one mile ahead of their troops to
detect any enemy activities during the snow storms.
About one half mile ahead on this road, in the hamlet,
enemy movement was spotted.
The tank and riflemen set off a few rounds, but due to
poor visibility, casualties were not verified. One of the
enemy raised his hands and walked towards the
American troops to surrender.
As the GIs searched him for arms or documents, his inner
clothing consisted of a North Korean officer's uniform.
They sent him back under guard to the division G2 for
interrogation. The storm increased and I left the unit,
which was north of Ami-Dong in Korea. 7th Infantry
Division. 7th Gig. Co. Photo Sect.   6 March 1951

Cpl. Charles E. Frye, CO M, 32nd Rct, 7th Inf. Div. stands guard over a POW of the 9th North Korean Division. He is being interrogated by Capt. Richard M. Lally (Cairo, Ill) KMAG – 7th ROK Division at Ami-Dong, Korea. American GI's from Korean Army watch this event. 1 March 1951

POWs during a siege hide behind a massive sand bag wall as the enemy shells our position.

MARINES MARCH POWs
As 7th Infantry Division troops advance to Han River to cross into Seoul, Korea. U.S. marines bring in captured North Koreans to POW Camp south of Seoul, Korea.
Sept 1950

A POW tagged Officer (left) and North Korean enlisted soldiers wait for trucks to take them to a POW Stockade south of Seoul, Korea. 7th. Inf. Div. troops captured quite a few enemy combatants.
Sept 1950

A well-clad (for North Korean troops) officer stands with his enlisted soldiers as they wait to be trucked to stockades in rear of fighting going on in Seoul, Korea.
The 7th Inf. Div. troops sent prisoners to the rear for questioning.

Sept. 1950

A GI and a KATUSA stand by as a psychologist war officer has a Chinese POW scan the papers. This was before using the loud speaker system on the vehicle to talk to his fellow Chinese in the hill to surrender. This was near The 7th Inf. Div. front lines.

North Korean
POWs are
guarded as
they await UN
transportation
to hospital and
then to
guarded areas.

A 7th Inf. Div. photographer records
this event for U.S. History files - North
Korean POW's outside of Seoul, Korea
captured by 7th Inf. Div.

Hundreds of North Korean prisoners are being marched back by UN Troops. They were captured in the fierce fighting for Seoul, Korea. Sept 1950

Two villagers are being questioned by troops for information on the whereabouts of the enemy.

An older North Korean soldier, just after the medics fumigated him for body lice, is photographed in a 7th Infantry Division area. Captured by members of the divisions' infantrymen, he will be interrogated by intelligence officers and then sent to a UN prisoner of war stockade.
The tattered winter uniform that he is wearing did not protect him from the sub-zero temperatures, especially when it got wet.

April 1951

A truck load of "Red" prisoners are guarded by one of the divisions Katusa Soldiers. They are headed to the rear to be questioned by 7th Inf. Div. intelligence.

UN Guards march large groups of POWs to their camp.

A young North Korean POW was captured by The 7th Inf. Div. This photo shows that the North Korean Military drafted youngsters to fight against the Yankees (and also any oldster that could fight).

Pete & POW

Hill 902 Ip-Tong was littered with enemy clothing, grenades, rifles, etc.

Cpl. Robert Peterson 7th Signal Company 7th Infantry Division left his camera at the top of the hill and borrowed a rifle to cover me as we went down the hill. As we came back up the hill, "Pete" hollered to take his picture. I spun around and "Pete" was leading a North Korean up the hill to members of "A" Company, 32nd RCT to hold him for G2.

Then Peterson picked up his camera and we photographed the massive amount of equipment and dead left by the enemy in the nightlong fight to dislodge the GIs. **THEY FAILED!!**

24 April 1951

32nd RCT, 7th Division EX USA POW Cpl. James H. Ransier (Leroy, NY) & Pvt. Donald L. Faudskar (Silverton, Ore.), members of the 32nd RCT, 7th Division Infantry, are carried by medics to an Aid station behind the front lines after being released by a North Korean Colonel near Paegchpo-Ri, Korea.

Ransier & Faudskar rest
Cpl. James H. Ransier (Leroy, NY) & Pvt. Donald L.
Faudskar (Silverton, Ore.), members of the 32nd
RCT, 7th Division Infantry wait with other GIs from
the patrol for medics to check them out and bring
them to an Aid station.
They had some GI rations, the first after their 10
days as prisoners, courtesy of the photographer.

32nd RCT, 7th Division EX USA POW Cpl. James H.
Ransier (Leroy, NY) & Pvt. Donald L. Faudskar
(Silverton, Ore.), members of the 32nd RCT, 7th
Division Infantry, hold the safe conduct pass given to
them by a North Korean Colonel.
The pass was to show to any North Korean troops
that stopped them in their walk back to American
Lines; to allow them to continue.

REFUGEES

A grandmother tries to comfort her child as we were able to keep their village safe from the enemy. The poor children had to play in the rubbish.

Entire families displaced by the war check their belongings as a child plays in the street. Another child is bundled up near some of the luggage.

Hundreds of South Korean families displaced by the War evade death with our protection. The enemy kept coming south and we slowly, with the South Korean Army, sent them back North.

A Korean civilian washes clothes in a stream beside the shadow of a blown up bridge at Sinpung-Ni, Korea. Engineers of Co B 13th combat engineers battalion, 7th Infantry Division work on repairing the structure to permit combat troop vehicles to continue their drive north to the 38th parallel. The enemy had blown the bridge to hinder the forward progress of the 7th. Division combat troops.

7 April 1951

Refugees who left their villages as the enemy approached wait by the roadside as American GIs come up to force the enemy back.

At times in our area we would see a few people or streams of people fleeing their homes as the enemy approached. Most of the people that stayed were killed by the enemy.

The 7th Inf. Div. saw Korean Refugees washing clothes near the Central Front in May 1951. We saw families everywhere as they were displaced by the North Koreans.

Some South Korean family wagons were loaded with lots of their home goods as they fled to the South. The 7th Inf. Div. troops were chasing the North Korean after they "Bugged Out".

Hundreds of refugees carrying all they could salvage, leaving their homes behind as massive Chinese Forces level their village. A few ROK Soldiers march south with them. Many roads were clogged by South Korean civilians fleeing North Korean attacks. 7th Inf. Div. troops chased the North Koreans back.

Thousands of South Korean families flee south on shattered foot bridges that helped them cross rivers and streams as the 7th Division troops advance northward.

War time did not stop women in small villages in many zones from working food areas.
As the 7th Inv. Div. troops moved after the retreating North Korean enemy,
North Korean troops "Bugged Out" to evade combat with the 7th.

Refugees are held up in field so that 7th Infantry Division Foot soldiers and motorized vehicles can advance up towards Seoul. Refugees were heading south to evade capture or death by the North Koreans.

RICE'S RAIDERS

Rice's Raiders, or in Korean, "The Benedae Group", was a relatively unknown band of anti-guerrilla group in the division. Formed by G2 to conduct behind the lines activities, Capt. Robert L. Rice was the leader of the group that included at one time Sgt. Yashita Koba (Corenada, CA), Sgt. Robert Smisek (St. Paul, MN) and a couple of other American GIs. Sorry I forgot their names over the years.

A South Korean Police Chief, Lt. Col. Pak Chong Jun was assistant to Capt. Rice and a North Korean, Kim Jung Ki was known as Leader Kim. Since 1945, he led guerrilla activities with a 60-man band against the communists around Pungsan. Wounded twice and captured, he escaped to the mountains. The Communists then killed his family.

Rice's Raiders was formed with over 100 Koreans, both North & South to conduct raids behind enemy lines and secure arms and information that were turned into G2. Small and large groups of the "Benedae's" would leave Rice's base, cross frozen rice paddies in single file, climb mountains, and attack the enemy in their own camps or set up ambushes.

I spent 7 days behind enemy lines, recording on film their activities, plus pulling my share of guard duty. I was later awarded the Army Commendation Medal with Metal Pendant for my coverage of the unit; both in their home camps and patrols.

Rice's Raiders were always alert and helped the 7th Inf. Div. often. Guard tower in a village.

Sgt. Smisek checks for further orders.

North Korean schoolhouse burns on the outskirts of village. Rice's raiders leveled it as it was a stronghold for the enemy. They made sure no enemy was still setting up the enemy for the advanced 7th Inf. Div. troops.

A North Korean enemy stronghold Village
House was leveled and left to burn to the
ground by Rice's Raiders unit and 7th Inf. Div.

A highly ranked South Korean Officer assigned to our division studies documents about our movements. He was one of the leaders of Rice's Raiders.

Checked out an enemy home - we took their weapons and burned the house.

The lowest temperature in our area was 32 degrees
below. Rice's Raiders tank go on motorized patrol 15
miles ahead of 7th Div. infantry lives. This tank was
loaned by the 7th Inf. Div. unit as Rice's Raiders were
never officially issued tanks.

Most villagers always helped our 7th division troops and
"The Raiders" with good information with the division.
Another patrol is getting info from villagers.

**Receiving my Army Commendation Medal for days
behind enemy lines with Rice' Raiders**

**We tangled nearly daily with the enemy deep into
their lines. Our objective was to find out where their
supplies and men were and to decimate them. We
more than often did.**

Rice's Raiders burned down enemy house

Rice's Raiders interrogate the enemy.

Rice's Raiders readying for secret mission

Rice's Raiders Burning Enemy Held Village House

Photographers are NUTS! Nobody that sane would photograph enemy action in war, when his eye is focused on an image in his camera. He cannot scan the horizon for enemy movement, as an Infantryman can. I was in that category. Later in Nam, Bob Lafoon proved I was a nut. When the 7th Infantry Division evacuated North Korea in December due to the tremendous inflect of Chinese manpower, we regrouped in the southern section of South Korea and advanced northwards, now better equipped and armed.

When we and other U.N. Forces left, ships were loaded with many, many thousands of North Koreans. fleeing their own and Chinese forces. Hundred upon hundreds in our division area begged to be armed and fight with U.S. units to liberate their country. They were screened.

A new arrival to the 7th Infantry Division G-2 Section was Capt. Robert Rice of Evansville Indiana. An idea was formed in the division for an anti guerrilla band, led by Capt. Rice, three U.S. enlisted men and a Col. Pok, a South Korean police chief. After many days and hours of hard training, the unit went on many patrols, behind enemy lines. When I heard they were going deep into enemy land, the photo officer reluctantly let me go with them. Moving in after dark, we spent a week behind their lines, getting info, and stalking and capturing enemy forces. There were no losses to our group. Sometimes we hid in caves in the forests. I felt perfectly safe. Upon leaving the unit, the leader, Leader Kim, a North Korean defector presented me the Russian burp gun (the photo on the back cover) that he had captured from an enemy agent. He told me he would die before I was captured. The unit was approximately 140 men strong, but smaller units went on these missions. The nit was named in honor of Cpt. Rice as Rice' Raiders or in Korean, the Benadae group. This pic was taken on return to our lines. I was pooped! Later on through the approval of Captain Rice I was awarded the Army Commendation Medal with Metal Pendant. This took place in the early Spring of 1951.

Rhode Islander with Guerrillas

Patrol of Rice's Raiders Ferrets Reds Behind Lines

Captain Says Army Can Use Tactics on Wider Scale in Korea

A former Providence Journal-Bulletin newsboy, who is serving with the Seventh Infantry Division as a correspondent in Korea, accompanies a patrol that picks up Communist spies who lead Rice's Raiders to a Red stronghold. This is the last of three articles.

By CPL. CHARLES W. DUMAS

FARMHOUSE IN FLAMES: While two of his friends stand at the ready, a Benedae patrol scout braves flames to search for possible trapped occupants.

— U.S. Army Photos by Sgt. Pete Rogness

HUNTING PARTY: A patrol from Rice's Raiders strikes out toward one of the many mountain passes the unit favors in conducting surprise forays against Korean Communists.

Published photos of Rice's Raiders

RIFLES

As the Anti-Tank and Mine Platoon, 17th Infantry
RCT was moving north, heavy sniper fire from the
North Koreans forced them to take cover by the side
of a sandy hill.
The squad leader SGT. Howard S. Roberts from
Waltham, Mass., opens fire on visible targets.
While he fires at the enemy movements on the hills
just forward of his position, an American Major in
back of him surveys the horizon for other enemy
held positions.
Three South Korean soldiers hug the sides of their
concealment in fear. None of them had brought
clips of ammo with them. None could return fire.
A half track moved up later and with their firing
power softened up the enemy fire and the unit soon
continued on their northward objective. The
skirmish took place in the Yachon-Ni area in Korea.

16 April 1951

A 7th Inf. Div. rifleman is on the crest returning fire as he spotted an enemy target.

7th Inf. Div. returns fire as a radio man is receiving instructions from front line spotters.

A 7th Infantry G.I. fires at movement as enemy troops flee the American troops that are advancing towards the burning town.

L-R Cpl. Thomas E Bullis (Troy, NY) gunner, and PFC Charles R Gilman (Peoria, IL) asst. gunner, fire 57mm recoilless rifle at enemy pillbox during action against the Chinese Communist forces at bottom of hill 860 near Kaoch Ang-Ni, Korea. 24 Apr 1951

An unidentified Member of the 17TH RCT, 7TH Infantry Division fires his 30 cal Carbine. He spotted the enemy on an opposite hill to the one that his company had just taken without opposition.

The infantrymen were relaxing, smoking and laughing. Suddenly heavy small arms and machine gun fire opened up spraying the entire hillside near Oron-Ni, Korea.

The firing got so intense that he crawled to a more concealed position before I could get his information for my captions.

5 April 1951

While talking to a 7th Division photographer, and reloading clips with ammo, PFC John F. Paige (Savannah, GA), 7th Reconnaissance Battalion, 7th Infantry Division placed his helmet on the top othe gully that he was using for concealment. A burst of burp gun fire blew the helmet by his feet. Three bullet holes found their target. But, no head was in it. He is returning the fire at Yachow-Ni, Korea.

He asked a nearby SGT. with his unit if he could take the helmet home when he rotated, and was told, "Kid, if you make it OK, keep the pot."

16 April 1951

ENEMY ARMS

One 7th Infantry Division Company gathered all of these
enemy arms & equipment after a savage all night battle.
They found more in their chase of the enemy.

Infantrymen and spotters take cover and return heavy
fire against the North Korean Army. The same GIs were
bunched up as there were very few sections on the hill for
protection.

I COVERED A SOUTH KOREAN WAC TRAINING PROGRAM AT
A BASE IN KOREA. A REGULAR KOREAN ARMY OFFICER
HELPS A KOREAN WAC SOLDIER IN CORRECT STANCE FOR
HITTING TARGET.   So. KOREA 1962

    PHOTO BY: S/SGT. PETER "RUPY" RUPLENAS

"RUPY"

Peter R Ruplenas

The division photo officer had me stand on a tank holding camera and binoculars for a "Hometown GA in combat" release for a Boston, Mass paper.

After he left, two of his enlisted reporters said his pose "sucked". So, unwrapping 4 rolls of my 35-mm Mopic film all over me, they took a couple pics. One was used in the Boston Globe, and weeks later two of my "Southie" neighbors wrote and both said I haven't 'changed' and look as crazy as ever.

Incidentally, the film was from WWII stock with a 1945 expiration date. Couldn't use except training. This scan was done from a Xerox photo, the original was stolen.

This was with the 7th Inf. Div. 7th Signal photo lab

**35mm
and
MOPIC
camera**

**A few
clicks from
the front
lines.
I look at a
dead
South
Korean
that was
killed by
an enemy
unit.**

229

All set to move out with the 7th with my camera and weapon.
A few officers in the various units asked me to shave and take the "Rupy" off of my hat.
I told them no and said the Division Commanding Officer told me I could leave them both on and "shoot" my good films.

Autographed by fellow Combat photographers Lee Dell and Hunkins both with the 7th Signal CorpsPhotographers

PHOTOGRAPHER ON RIGHT, SP. PETER "RUPY" RUPLENAS, 8TH ARMY PHOTOG, WAITS FOR THE CEREMONIES TO START AGAIN AT 8TH ARMY HEADQUARTERS IN SEOUL, KOREA. IT WAS LOADED WITH BIG BRASS FROM THROUGHOUT KOREA.

I am hiding in a bushy area as the enemy opened up on my unit as we were advancing.

Fall 1950

The "photo lab gang". Two GIs from the Division and two of my cameramen enjoy a cake that my wife Hazel sent to me from Japan for my birthday.

Needless to say we all enjoyed that cake!

Captain Robert Flint (rear left) and his Photo Unit of still and MOPIC cameramen. Taken before we spread out to cover various combat troops.

"To Sgt Peter Ruplenas, The zaniest (and I am not kidding) of all the 7th Division shutterbugs. From Pusan to Hyesanjin and back always plenty of laughs and <u>never</u> a dull moment. Your pix always made my stories look better. Thanks & good luck Your Pal Charlie "Bud" Dumas"

I watch as two soldiers shake hands near the front line before the 7th Div. troops take the mountains in back which were held by North Korean troops. The hill was secured by Americans a few hours later. Spring 1951

Cpt. Robert Flint, 7th Inf Div Signal Company photo officer fires his 45 cal pistol at a boulder over 100 yards across the river. He showed me that if any photographers are pinned down, they can return enemy firepower and keep them away until infantry help arrives. There were times when division photographers were fired at while moving towards troops or returning. A Katusa stands by, while an infantryman checks results.

Cpl. Thompkins (Lake George, NY) and I pose for pic on D-Day Plus One at Inchon before Photographic 7th Infantry Division in their advance north.

September 1950

During a break in the action near the front line, my buddy and I enjoy a full meal from an Army Mess Cup.

Everyone loved listening to my big radio as we went to Japan from Korea

Documenting the 7th Inf. Div. action while in South Korea.

The destruction was done by the North.

235

My fellow combat photographer and I pose in front of "Flints Flop House Photo Lab". We put the name on the tent.

Full Class A uniform 8th Army Unit

Some "wise" officer wanted to know how we developed our films and prints. So I showed him our "lab", he left very annoyed!

GIs Coffee Kimpo 7ᵗʰ Inv. Div headquarters - P.I.O. enlisted men and Rupy try cups of Java to keep themselves warm at the Kimpo Airbase, while waiting for further movement orders.
We moved forward the following day.

1950

High on top of a mountain in Seoul Korea.

GOD BLESS OUR HOME

After sending their film and captions off to Tokyo by
air, CPL. Wilfred Hunkins, on the right, and myself both
combat cameramen with the 7th Infantry Division Signal
Company, relax in a warm "hooch" at HYSEN-JIN, north
Korea on the banks of the Yalu river. Reading and
relaxing also is a member of the 17th RCT that secured
the town.

With "rental" units hard to find, the two cameramen
found this "mansion" and put a claim on it.
With a hot fire going in the 55 gallon drum stove, and
coffee warming up, the three men were safe from the
Siberian winds and the below zero temperature.

22 November 1950

Cpl. Hunkins on left and myself in our warm tent.
The first thing we do upon returning from the front is to
get our captions, stories and film from the day's activities
wrapped and dropped off at an airbase for shipment to
GHC in Tokyo for processing. Then hot chow and relax by
candlelight; weapons and cameras at the ready. We are
with the 7th Signal Company, 7th Inf. Div. in North Korea.

A fellow
cinematographer
and me before
moving up to
document the 7th
Inf. Div. troops
facing the enemy.

239

My Christmas tree in Japan

TOP combat photographer with the 7th Division in Korea, Sgt. Peter R. Ruplenas will shortly report to Fort Monmouth, N. J., as an instructor. He is shown above with the cameras he used during eight months in combat. Rupy was first photog to reach Hysenjin on the Manchurian border. He was officially rated tops over all other Signal Corps photogs in April, after holding third place from January on.

My personal favorite photo of me in Korea

While on assignment for 8th Army CQ, I went on games of U.S. and South Korean. I pose with a top S.K. naval office just before we dove. S.K. P.T. boats got ready to dive bomb us.

Photo Officer Robert Flint (center front row next to me), our Lab, Still & MOPIC Team, along with our mascot

241

7th Inv. Div headquarters P.I.O. enlisted men and Rupy try cups of Java to keep themselves warm at the Kimpo Airbase, while waiting for further movement orders

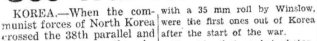

Combat Cameramen See War At Worst

KOREA.—When the communist forces of North Korea crossed the 38th parallel and invaded South Korea the mission of combat photographers in this war had begun. Lt. Frank Winslow and Sgt. Thomas Anderson, Korean Military Advisory Group Signal Corps photographers, were right on the spot and for two days were the only official photographers covering the situation. Motion picture and still men of GHQ photographic lab arrived at Suwon and went into action under fire immediately.

These photographers are assigned to A Company, 71st Signal Service Battalion, Headquarters and Service Group, and they have been covering every phase of the struggle in Korea since June 27. Until the arrival of Eighth Army and commercial photographers, these GHQ men along with Winslow and Anderson had the field to themselves.

First of the A Company men in Korea were Sgt. Ray Turnbull and Cpl. John Romanowski, whose still and motion pictures, along with a 35 mm roll by Winslow, were the first ones out of Korea after the start of the war.

The risks that combat photographers take daily often exceed those of the infantryman who is properly armed to defend himself. A man with a camera "glued" to his eye is a sitting duck for an enemy sniper or an enemy patrol.

Combat pictures cannot be taken from a foxhole! GHQ men who can vouch for that are Lt. Edward Plummer, Cpl. Paul G. Hampton, Cpl. John J. Thomas and PFC Edward M. Crone, who were wounded in Korea. Lt. Plummer still has several weeks of hospitalization ahead. Other Signal Corps photographers have been wounded recently.

Present Army organization provides a photographic team within each division. When the division engages the enemy, the still and motion picture cameras "fire" side by side with infantry, artillery and armored weapons.

Not always attached to ground units, GHQ photographers have carried out missions aboard ships of the UN naval forces and in Air Force and Navy planes on combat missions. Messages of appreciation testify to the quality of their work.

Still pictures, in addition to the hundreds of official uses, are viewed by public information representatives and a great number are selected for release to publications all over the world.

This article could not be complete without bowed honor to those six valiant photographers killed in action: Lt. Roy T. Riggs, Sgt. Alex Rolex, Cpl. Edmond A. Kiezanowski, Cpl. Richard E. Millis, PFC Myron P. Marble and PFC John Corey.

243

u.s.Lady

75¢ • MAY 1963

POST OF THE MONTH
SEOUL, KOREA
Who says it's a hardship tour?

THE HOWLING SUCCESS OF
HELOISE
Her household hints column
brought 250,000 requests
for one rug cleaning booklet

PLUS an exotic recipe
for Korean sinseulo---
served from a tabletop
fire pot!

SWINGING:
Korean girls have done
it for centuries

SEOUL, KOREA

By Lynn Tillman

U. S. Army photos by Sp5 Peter Ruplenas

Ancient palaces and royal gardens are among Seoul's most treasured relics of an exotic past. Pausing at the edge of a lotus pond during an early spring sightseeing tour (l. to r.) are: Mrs. Roe, wife of Lt. Col. Murray Roe, USMC; Mrs. Merrifield, wife of Maj. Leslie R. Merrifield, USAF, and Mrs. Steele, wife of Maj. Leonard H. Steele, USAF. In the background is the pleasure pavilion of one of Korea's last queens.

Liz Custer, they say, was the gal who first pointed out to her sisters-behind-the-uniform that it's not only possible but much better to follow the old boy around in his travels, even into Injun territory, than to sit safely at home and wonder what's happening to him—or what he's up to. We're with her.

But there are apparently a few people back home who view orders to Korea with the same alarm as early Easterners viewed the prospect of Mama's starting West when a calvaryman went out to protect the settlers and wanted her to go along. If the lady herself wasn't shaken up at the notion, it's a sure bet that her kith and kin painted fearsome pictures of what awaited her—and it's the same today.

Many of our voyagers now happily settled here in Korea are still talking about the fit Mother and Father threw at the idea of daughter's coming to this forsaken spot to perch on a snow-covered mountain and chop her own firewood, while watching for Peter Lorre characters sneaking out from behind the rocks. And as for bringing the children! Oh, my dear.

Several circumstances contributed to the idea of Korea's being The Hardship Tour. First, the military itself began referring to it that way, meaning only that every man must do a

thirteen-month tour out here without his family. And actually, that is the only *real* hardship involved. Also, men who had been in Korea in combat told horrendous tales of conditions here, and of course these were true at the time. But the idea was contagious and snowballed. Now even those who begin counting the days left in their tour the minute they step off the plane will admit when pinned down that living conditions here are more than adequate. As for the ladies—any who fuss about being in Korea with the whole family together should make an early appointment at the mental health clinic.

There are four places in Korea where service families are permitted and accommodated: Seoul, Pusan, Taegu, and with the Navy at Chinhae. Seoul has by far the largest group of dependents because it is headquarters for all the elements in Korea: Eighth Army, Korea Military Advisory Group (KMAG), Provisional Military Assistance Advisory Group—Korea (PROVMAAG-K), U. S. Forces Korea (USFK), the Air Force and Navy Advisory Groups, as well as United Nations Command (UNC). KMAG also has detachments at the other two cities, where there are smaller housing compounds and facilities similar to ours here in the capital.

Surrounded by culture 4000 years old, many military wives take advantage of a Korean tour to improve artistic abilities or develop latent talents. Mrs. Harry Sanborn, a member of the Oriental classical painting group, watches intently as artist Bong Chae Ko demonstrates a brush stroke. Ko is a member of the faculty at the Academy of Fine Arts, Seoul. He studied painting and philosophy in China and is a noted master of his art.

KOREAN GEOGRAPHY AND HISTORY

Korea, as you can see on any map, is a peninsula, with Manchuria and Siberia to the north, the Yellow Sea on the west, and the Sea of Japan and Japan itself to the east and southeast. It is a mountainous country generally, and only about one-fifth of it is arable, with most of the agriculture carried on in the south. Since North Korea was the great industrial area, the division of the country has meant that the southern people have had a slow climb toward economic prosperity and still have a long way left, but they are making great progress.

The climate compares to that of the region between Georgia and Maine in many respects. Ordinarily Korea has a distinct rainy season in the summer, and July, August and early September are hot and humid. Winters in the Seoul area and north are very cold and quite dry; in the south, Pusan and Chinhae have somewhat milder temperatures.

Spring and fall are delightful, with pleasantly warm days and cool nights. Like many parts of our own country, Korea in winter looks drab and bleak and colorless, but from spring until late fall the rice paddies cover the country with emerald, and even the rugged, forbidding mountains turn green. The areas toward the south become especially lush and appear almost tropical, a strange contradiction in a country that definitely is not.

The Korean people trace the origin of their nation back about 43 centuries, since on the ancient calendar 1963 is the year 4296. It is believed that the basic population derived from a succession of migrations from North China through the Korean peninsula over a period of thousands of years. From the Chinese

16

ROK WACs are conspicuous for their smart appearance. Colonel Thompson watches approvingly as a recruit adjusts the tilt of her cap at an outdoor mirror in the barracks area.

Two Korean WACs perform one of their Corp's most important duties—broadcasting messages over a loud speaker at a forward position near the Demilitarized Zone. Teams of women soldiers take turns telling the Republic's story to Communist North Korean troops on the other side.

Regular infantry officers teach marksmanship to ROK WACs. Emphasis is not placed on combat training, but WACs in potentially explosive Korea must know how to handle firearms.

nickel have to be built in to coincide with accurate comprehension of their terms of money. "It takes a lot of practice," Colonel Thompson says, "but we have a lot of fun doing it."

To accustom them to typical stateside surroundings, Colonel Thompson takes her charges through a well planned series of social events, luncheons, receptions, evening parties and formal and informal events. They also make frequent trips to the movies shown on post and take meals in the officers mess hall. Dining in a predominantly male mess hall is, in the beginning, something of a novelty to the ROK WAC but under Colonel Thompson's gentle tutelage their shyness gradually wears away and is replaced by a modest glow of confidence.

Although the organizational structure and operating procedures of the ROK WAC parallel those of the U.S. WAC, many of its problems are different. For one thing, the ROK Corps has had to fight harder for recognition and full acceptance than its American counterpart. Revered customs firmly restricting the usefulness of women to inspirational and purely domestic pursuits are far from forgotten in a land with a 4000-year-old cultural heritage. Born at the height of the Korean conflict, the ROK WAC has survived by consistently demonstrating its practical value, hewing firmly to the highest standards of conduct and never relaxing its determination. During the nine years since the cessation of hostilities it has steadily improved its status as an integral and respected branch of its country's armed forces.

In 12 years of existence it has trained a total of 5,941 women of whom 128 have become officers. In common with the U.S. WAC it concentrates on teaching enlisted women typing, switchboard and communication equipment operation, and clerical and administrative duties. But because of the proximity of the Communist enemy it takes on many other assignments not currently within the scope of its American counterpart.

Utilizing the woman's touch, teams of ROK WACs climb the precipitous peaks in the Demilitarized Zone and speak for hours over huge amplifiers facing out over Communist lines. "We know that they are heard on the other side and that they have some effect because the Communists make furious efforts to drown them out."

Because of the relatively small size of the ROK WAC and the very large numbers of Korean young women eager to join, recruitment is a somewhat different matter. Officers face a great responsibility in making the right selections from among thousands of qualified candidates. This situation has an effect on discipline also. ROK WAC officers can afford to be very severe but seldom need to be for every girl in the corps knows there are at least 100 others waiting to take her place at the first sign of unfitness.

Colonel Thompson, who completed 20 years of military service in August 1962, came to Korea from Ft. McPherson last May. Since 1947, with the exception of a three-year stint in recruitment, her military career had been in intelligence. The role of advisor, however, is neither new nor strange to her since she was trained as an educator and before joining the U.S. WAC, taught in the public school system of Howland, Ohio. Colonel Thompson expects to bid good-bye to her many Korean friends later this month and return to the States for a new assignment in Washington. ★★★

U. S. LADY

247

SEOUL
DESTRUCTION

The glorious Capitol building, Seoul, Korea gutted by North Korean & UN firepower.
This is what the 7th Infantry Division combat troops saw after crossing the Han River.
The North Koreans from June occupied the capital until the UN forces drove them out in September.
The communist gutted this splendid building's interior, and the exterior was pot marked by UN firepower.
26 Sept 1950

Businesses and houses are tightly packed together in peacetime Seoul

Inside the Capital Building in Seoul. Very little damage was done to this building but it was completely gutted.

In 1957 the Seoul Capitol Building is still bombed out.
I shot these on special assignment for the 8th Army headquarters.

One of the busy sites travelling along in Seoul

This department store was one of the largest in Seoul, Korea. Blocks of buildings gutted by Firepower but this one was not completely gutted. September 1950

Block after block of industrial zones of city are completely destroyed, Seoul, Korea.

As I entered Seoul with elements of the 7th Infantry Division, I was shocked by the devastation that I saw while walking with the troops.

Factories, stores and homes were completely destroyed, leaving nothing for the people. Air strikes and artillery caused the damage. The total destruction was done by the United Nations and the Communist forces in the seesaw battles before the city was finally captured by the UN forces.

The city was devoid of the civilian population, except for a few civilians that we saw during the day, walking in a Zombie-like state along the debris in downtown streets.

27 September 1950

View of Seoul from top of damaged Capitol Building

7ᵗʰ Inf. Div. enters parts of Seoul Korea after artillery damage by enemy.   September 1950

Block after block of industrial zones of city are completely destroyed. Elements of 7ᵗʰ Inf. Div. were the first troops to reach and occupy Seoul, Korea.

Sept 1950

A Shrine in the Capitol area stands tall without any damage from the War.

There was bitter fighting around the Main Railroad Station.

This photo taken in 1957.

The Koreans are called the "Irish of The East" for their strong work ethic and I agree with that.

Downtown "Skid Row" near Camp Coiner 1957

259

UNC Honor Guard Kimpo Airbase Seoul Korea

Camp Schimmel at Sunset Nov 1955

SHIPS and SUBS

A ship, loaded with troops, heads for a dock in Korea to unload troops and cargo.

American Navy and Army brass talk to a dignitary at port.

Before Diving on Submarine in Korean Waters, a Military Attaché checks out the ship's search lights.

American and South Korean big brass are briefed deep in the heart of a US sub by a sub officer while submerged in Inchon Harbor.   1962

CHINHAE HARBOR, KOREA, 1962
3 HIGH RANKING MILITARY & CIVILIAN
ON CONING TOWER OF U.S. SUB MINUTES
BEFORE WE DOVE. So. KOREAN P.T. BOATS
ATTACKED SUB BEFORE & AFTER WE
CRASH DIVED.
IT WAS DURING NAVAL WAR GAMES BETWEEN
U.S. AND KOREAN NAVAL FORCES.

PHOTO BY
S/SGT. PETER "RUPY" RUPLENAS

Dive! Dive! I took this picture from the top of the U.S.
Sub in Inchon, Harbor seconds before the dive.   1962

US sailors scan horizon for attacking South Korean P.T. boats in war games in Chinnae Harbor, South Korea. They are on the U.S.S. Queenfish.

1962

U.S.S. QUEENFISH
My 1st SVC CEVISE
CHINHAE KOREA '62

SEOUL, KOREA, October 30, 1962 (United Nations Command) -- --
Inter-Communications Fireman Apprentice Norbert L. Konieczny mans
a lookout post aboard the USS Queenfish during the vessel's visit
to the Chinhae Naval Base. The submarine was in the Republic of
Korea conducting anti-submarine warfare exercises with elements of
the ROK Navy. (OFFICIAL US ARMY PHOTO) BY

-30- S/SGT. PETER P.
RUPLENAS

A U.S. NAVY CHIEF SUPERVISES TRAINING OF
TWO So. KOREAN NAVY ENLISTED MEN IN THEIR
WORK ON ONE OF ~~THEIR~~ THEIR SHIPS ENGINES.
THE U.S. NAVY HAS A CREW OF SAILORS STATIONED
AT THE SOUTH KOREAN NAVY BASE IN CHINHAE, S.K.
TO TRAIN THE S.K's!
SUMMER 62

PHOTO BY:
S/SGT. PETER "RUPY"
RUPLENAS

**US
Naval
Officer
Foundry
Workers
Pusan
Korea**

**War Games
Chinhae
Harbor. U.S.
sailor waits
forward on his
sub to welcome
"Big Brass".
They later dove
when South
Korean PT
boats attack.
Summer 1962**

US Sailors lower a sea weapon in training.

US Sailors relax after a hard day of duty on a submarine in Japan.

U.S. SAILORS SUPERVISE A KOREAN NAVY
ENLISTED MAN AS HE WORKS ON A KOREAN
NAVY SHIP COMPONENT. THIS IS A THE KOREAN NAVY
BASE AT CHINHAE, So. KOREA. THE U.S. NAVY HAS
A DETATCHMENT HERE TO SUPERVISE AND TRAIN
So. KOREAN SAILORS.

SUMMER '63

PHOTO BY:
PETER
"RUPY"
RUPLENAS

SEOUL, KOREA, October 30, 1962 (United Nations Command) – –
Maj. Gen. Van H. Bond, Acting Chief of Staff, United Nations
Command, and Chief, Joint Military Assistance Advisory Group, Korea
(ProvMAAG-K) leads a group of US and Korean dignitaries aboard the
USS Queenfish at Chinhae Naval Base. The party remained aboard
while the submarine conducted anti-submarine warfare exercises with
elements of the ROK Navy. (OFFICIAL US ARMY PHOTO) BY :

S/SG. PETER "RUDY" RUPENAS

1962

With lifesavers on, US Sailors pull out of port.

273

Landing Operations Korea Sep 60

Leaving Chinhae Harbor USS Bream by PT Boat 10-62

I DON'T GIVE A DAMN IF HE IS ONE OF YOUR PHOTOGRAPHERS GENERAL. GET
HIM THE HELL OFF THE TORPEDOES.....

In Chinjae harbor - US Subs Military games

During U.S. Navy training in Inchon Harbor. Navy boats move up deep sea divers as they scout for enemy.   1962

TANKS

A 7th Inf. Div. tank moves up on the forward roads.

One of our tanks with our troops moves forward through a village to engage the enemy. The villagers were very nice and understood we were there to help them and not harm or kill them like the enemy.

Very well hidden with a net camouflaged tank near the DMZ. His unit would scan the horizon for the enemy before his troops would advance.

Our division takes shelter in ditches as the tanks saturate the mountains ahead where the enemy was.

Enlisted men of Company "B", 13 Combat Engineers,
7th Infantry Division works on another section of a
mountain road.

The retreating North Koreans use heavy explosives
as they blew out many sections of the road.
The lead tank and infantrymen wait. Logs, rocks,
boulders and dirt are used to repair the road for safe
advance of the GIs and their tanks.

The breaks in the pass were so bad that even a foot
soldier could not advance.   But with their expertise
and back breaking work by the engineers, the
troops advanced through the entire mountain pass
the same day.

The enemy, a large North Korean force, was
"bugging out" in the mountains south of Paegchpo-
Ri.

13 March 1951

Our tank division rolls through a village moving up to shell the enemy ahead.

A 2nd Ranger Company Tank along with The 7th Inf. Div. moves forward while the tank unit gives them firing power against the North Korean troops.

A 7th Infantry Division tank column and a GI patrol move forward on a frigid day. Men are well spread out so any enemy rifle or burp gun fire would not multiply possible deaths. With the rice paddies frozen solid, troops had to spread out more to advance and "Bug Out" the North Koreans

PFC KARL G KLEIN (Seattle, WA), a bar man of the 7th reconnaissance company, 7th US engineer div fires his weapon into a burning village, Yachon-Ni, Korea.
Enemy small arms fire hampered the advance of troops of the 7th Infantry Division near YACHON-NI.

16 April 1951

A 7th Infantry Division tank does the impossible.
It climbs up a steep hill to give firing power to GIs at the
summit. The tank's heavy gunfire cleared the hill ahead
of the GIs so they could continue their advance against
Chinese forces. A 15th AAA, 7th Infantry Division unit fires
at enemy troops that they spotted in the hills ahead of
the advancing troops.
The troops of the division's 17th RCT were forcing the
enemy to retreat north of Norumegi Korea.
The infantrymen said they were glad to have the heavy
firepower of the half-track's quad fifty guns, backing
them in their assault.   **7 April 1951**

**Our division tankers
move forward to give
UN troops support from
the enemy.**

From his gun position on M-4 tank, Cpl. Henry J Karasek (Davenport, IA) gunner, 32nd Heavy Tank Co, 7th Infantry Division watches for enemy movement during action against the Chinese Communist forces near Yonhwadong, Korea   24 April 1951

A&B Companies 17th RCT with tank support advance N.E. towards Kumma-Ri.   Feb 1951

An M-4 tank of the 32nd RCT, U.S. Infantry Division (in background), immediately after it hit an antitank mine on a road in Korea. The blast of the exploding mine knocked over a U.S. Signal Corps photographer passing by, who took this picture as he regained his feet. The only damage caused by the explosion was that the tank's left track was blown off.   28 Feb 1951

EM of 13th Engineers, 7th Div. take cover in gully as enemy Anti-Tank gun opens up on a 32nd RCT, 7th Div. tank near Chaejae Korea. Shortly after this 7TH Inf. Div. cleared the area and we moved forward.   2 March 51

Here I am photographing my Division by a tank.

A Korean family cleared off the road so an armored thrust by 32 RCT could advance against the enemy in Ami-Dong Korea.   **March 1951**

While 7th Infantry Division moves up, 13th combat engineers prepare to fill road so tanks and other division's vehicles can move out to support infantrymen. Road was damaged by retreating enemy and further damaged by U.S. Air Force.

A 7TH Inf. Div. Tank column moves forward to provide heavy fire against the enemy so the infantry could move up.

Twin Ack Ack Guns of a 7th Infantry Division unit soften up a hillside prior to an infantry attack. The infantry spotters watch the results of the tank hits on enemy sites. Air Force jets and Army saturated the hill for an hour, but when the Infantrymen started an advance, the well dug enemy fired back. Shortly after 7TH Inf. Div. units took the hill.   Winter 1951

Sgt. James E Ward (Nahma, MI) gunner with the 32nd heavy tank co, 7th Infantry Division, watches as the navy and marine fighter-bombers strafe enemy-held hill on edge of the village of Yonhwa-Dong, Korea. 24 April 1951

Tank Hit Mine

After taking some photos while riding on top of the leading tank, I walked ahead and turned to take a picture of the lead tank and infantry advancing.

The three engineers from the 13th Combat Engineer Battalion., missed one mine.

The left track of the tank rolled onto a mine and stopped the tank dead in its track.

One of the engineers said that I was knocked about ten feet back by the blast.

I sat up and took a photo.

All that they could see in the shot was a lot of debris flying around.

This photo, the second shot, shows an officer from the infantry column running up to check on his men and the damage.

Debris is still flying on the left and a point man is squatting down as he looks at the thrown tread on the tank.

The M4 tank was with the 32nd RCT, 7th Inf. Division. The tankers were shook up, but no injuries, and the infantry continued their assignment on the outskirts of Hadaewa, Korea.

28 Feb. 1951

An American 7TH Inf. Div. tank corps and tanker relax
before heading north to clear roads for division
infantrymen

As infantrymen of Company "A" 17th RCT, 7th Infantry Div.
begin assault up slopes of enemy held hill 860 near
village of Kaoch Ang-Ni, Korea. Men of the 17th heavy
tank Company, 7th Div. provide cover fire from their M-4
tanks.   24 Apr 51

Men and tanks of 17th RCT, 7th Div, wait while artillery shells soften up enemy positions on mountain North of Chechon Korea The jeep moved into the ditch to get more protection from incoming fire.   **19 Feb 51**

"Reno Babe II", a tank from the 7th Infantry Division regiment, 7th Infantry Division, fires at enemy troops in the town of Yachon-Ni, Korea. While the town burns, USAF Jets fire rockets into troops entrenched in hills near the town.   **16 April 1951**

While Cpl. John H. Russell (Donnellson, IA), right, welder with SV Co, 17th RCT, 7th Infantry Division, works to repair hatch cover hit by anti-tank rifle, 1st Lt. Joseph L McCoy (Baltimore, MD) Tank Commander, 17th RCT, 7th Infantry Division fires 50 cal machine gun from turret off his M-4 tank at enemy held hillside; during action against the communist forces near the village of Kaoch-Ni, Korea.

7th Infantry Division tows a battle-damaged tank across a stream for repair.

7th Infantry Division tank named "Cynthia" rumbles through a village in its advance on Seoul. A few South Koreans were still there after the North Koreans "Bugged Out" northward   Sept. 1950

"Kathleen" a 7th Infantry Division tank encounters a problem in turning around after a Han River crossing. This very steep hill was too narrow to turn wide at the time. Cpl. John Romanowski, a GHQ photographer stands by. River banks Seoul, Korea.   Sept 50

Tank of 32nd RCT, 7th Div. returns fire of enemy anti-tank gun located in hill near Chaejae Korea. Advancing GIs take cover in ditch on the left.   2 March 51

General David Barr inspects all tanks of the 7th Division. One tank in the recent battle could not pull back from the enemy. They were damaged by enemy fire and had to abandon the tank because they did not have the official tools to fix the damage and pull back to American Lines. Every tank in the division had full crews and all equipment. No tank could move up front until they were 100% equipped.

While the 7th Inf. Div. holds the line for a few days, a tank named "Patty's Palace" sets up home for a day or two

Tankers wait for USAF Jets to leave before they open up. Both USAF jets, then the tanks saturated hills and mountains.   The 7th Inf. Div. then took the hill.

I learned very fast to stand in back of the firing tanks. One time I stood in front of one and when it fired, I was thrown a few feet and got a severe headache. Between that and the Infantry shelling I now suffer deafness in both ears. Tanks of the 17th RCT, 7th Div, fire at enemy pillboxes in hills along the Choyang River, Korea to aid the infantrymen in crossing the stream.   9 April 51

7th Infantry Division Tankers and members of the div.'s Anti-Tank and Mine Platoon relax during a break in combat. Hot meals, coffee and especially "mail call" helped them relax from the horrors of war. They are resting off the road beside homes damaged or destroyed in the conflict.   Spring 1951

Top of Tank Mine Sweepers
Infantrymen from the 32nd RCT, 7th Infantry Division
was making a drive after a North Korean force.
The road had been heavily mined, so 13th Combat
Engineers were sweeping the roads for mines or booby
traps. Tanks lead the infantry towards their target.
I got on the lead tank and took this picture of the three
engineers sweeping the road, plus two infantry point
men.
They were going to pass through the village of
Hadaewa ahead and continue their pursuit past the
mountain range ahead   28 Feb. 1951

Members of the 13th Combat Engineers, 7th Division,
comb the road to Chaejae, Korea.   2 March 1951

Tanks of 32nd rct, 7th infantry div. return to Chaejae, then advance again.

Tanks on the run moving out to support our troops

US Army tank has trouble moving out of its present firing zone. It finally made it out on its own.

Men and tanks of 32nd RCT 7th Infantry Division slowly move up mountain pass in search of fleeing Reds. Bombed out roads were filled in no time by 7TH Inf. Div. engineers. This was done so that the tanks and foot traffic could move out and advance against the enemy.

14 Mar 1951

A column of tanks rolls forward in pursuit of the enemy. I am glad they were there as we were being fired upon by the enemy.

A tank named "RENO BABY" helps our troops advance. One of ours is peeking out for a better look.

Need Help?   OK, the tanks are on the way

A "Napalm"
tank surprises
the enemy with
a fireburst.

Members of Co F & G, 17th RCT, 7th Infantry Division, with tank support, advance unopposed to Morumegi, Korea, within two miles of the 38th Parallel. Unit is well spread out to minimize casualty count.   7 April 1951

This photo signed by my buddy says "To Rupy: The first to the border! Greetings from Hyesanjin (that's me in the middle) Hal Randall 17th RCT Nov 21 1950".
He was referring to himself with the "middle" remark and the Yalu River with the "First to the border".

TANKERS ON BREAK
What more do they need besides a safe trip home?
7th Infantry Division Tankers and members of the div.'s
Anti-Tank and Mine Platoon relax during a break in
combat.   **Spring 1951**

**Tanks advance
against the
enemy which
was not in sight
because you can
see our troops
with their heads
outside the tank.**

TANKS ON THE MOVE   **Men and tanks of 32nd RCT 7th Infantry Division slowly move up mountain pass in search of fleeing Reds.**   **14 Mar 1951**

This tank named "Frances" saturates the enemy with fire. Our infantry was very close to the action and the tanks had to stop several times to repel the enemy.

TRAINS

When the first soldiers reached the Manchurian border and the Yalu River at Hysanjin in North Korea, an infantryman with the 17th RCT, 7th Infantry Division told my fellow team mate that there was a large tunnel going under the river towards Manchuria. We entered the tunnel and many yards inside. In complete darkness was a Trans-Siberian Railroad locomotive.

We could not see any damage to the front from Air Force fighters, but the sides were peppered with large holes from the guns of the fighters.

That may have been why the train did not escape further into the tunnel or make it across the river to Manchuria.

My fellow cameraman took this photo by "walking" with the few flash bulbs that we had to light up the tunnel and train.

With ASA 100 film and a F4.7lens on the Speed Graphic, we were both surprised at the results.

Upon coming out of the tunnel, an officer from the G-2 section, and a couple of infantry Sergeants told us that the tunnel was not cleared of possible enemy, and the two of us were "Crazy Bastards" to enter it like we did.

Photo by: Cpt Wilfred Hunkins andS/Sgt. Peter "Rupy" Ruplenas7[th] Sig. Co. Photo Section

21 November 1950

An infantryman with the 17th RCT told my sidekick and me that there was a long tunnel that carried trains from Manchuria into North Korea and maybe we could get some good photos.

Cpt. Hunkins and I ventured over to the entrance. Photos were taken from the top of the tunnel embankment looking towards Manchuria, where the single rail line crosses a bridge.

The rails seemed to be in good shape, but the bridge in the background seemed to have some damage from Air Force attacks. Hysenjin, Korea

21 Nov. 1950

LOCOMOTIVE

A North Korean locomotive lies in ruins, off track due to firepower of U.S. Air Force Fighters.
This led to a tunnel near the North Korean border that ran to Manchuria.

WATER

Enlisted men from the 7th Infantry Division,17th RCT frantically try to dislodge their boat that is stuck on some rocks.

An engineer from their 13th Combat Engineer team gives a final shove and the boat proceeded across the river under heavy enemy fire. The hillside that they were going to assault had a concrete Russian built bunker on it.

Moments before American mortar and tank fire pounded the hill, but tank fire started again as incoming enemy fire hampered the various boat crossings. Other GI troops, gathering to cross, had to run for cover near two tanks as enemy sniper fire sprayed the area.

This action took place near Umyang-Ni in Korea.

9 April 1951

TRUCKS CROSS HAN RIVER
Convoys of 7th Infantry Division trucks are lined up
waiting for amphibious transportation across the Han
River. They are advancing to the North Korean border.
Sept. 1950

MOVING UP
Passing men of Company "A" 13th Combat Engineer BN,
7th Inf. Div. who are rolling log up toward road they are
widening for future vehicular traffic.
24 APR 51

GIs WAIT TO CROSS
7th Infantry Division GIs stand by for another craft to take them across the Han River. There were not any bridges for them to cross at that time.   Sept 1950

GIs with full packs on their backs cross a river after their bridges were destroyed by the enemy.

Infantrymen of Co "A" 17th RCT, 7th Inf. Div. move up toward their objective, enemy held Hill #860 as they continue assault against the Chinese Communist forces North East of Kaoch Ang-Ni, Korea.

Engineer, 13th combat engineer fortify shoulders of road to support heavy vehicles.

Combat photographers with the 7th Signal Company, 7th Infantry Division photograph them in ankle deep river stream. That is me in the river.

24 April 1951

WINTER

Men of the 17th RCT, 7th Infantry Division, near the
Manchurian Border, advance through the outskirts of
Hyesanjin, North Korea as their advance nears the border
and the Yalu River. Both sides of the narrow street had
sandbagged tunnels that ran a block long. Then another
tunnel ran another block.

All of the GIs had their weapons slung or cross-slung. If
an enemy soldier fired at them, many would have been
killed or wounded. None of the homes were checked
either. And no order was given by the NCD or officer in
charge of this unit to do so.

I walked up to the front of the column and joined the two
point men leading the unit. At least they had their BARs
'on the ready' and would not be caught by surprise.
Shortly after this picture was taken, the point men and I
stood on the snow and ice facing Manchuria. We were the
first three Americans to reach the Manchurian border.

Other units in the 7th Infantry Division and other divisions
claim they reached the border. But the 17th RCT was the
only unit in the Korean War to reach the border.

       21 November 1950

Members of the 2nd Ranger Company, (An All Black Unit, and a DAMN GOOD ONE TOO!), advance ahead of the front elements of the 17th RCT, 7th Infantry Division. The unit was called into service to support the division's advance against deeply dug in enemy positions. With some division tank support, the unit crossed the ice laden, frigid river, and routed the enemy with no resistance at all. The operation took place at CHUCHON-NI.

19 Feb 1951

7th Inf. Div. Infantryman flatten out on the snowy hill.
They were trying to evade enemy fire and no one got hit.

Elements of the 17th Infantry Regiment, 7th Infantry Division continue their advance against the communist enemy near KAPSAN, Korea. As they advance towards the Yalu River and the Manchurian border, the weather dropped many degrees below zero. The temperature was logged in at 32° below zero.

21 Nov. 1950

Amidst the ruins of the village of Ami-Dong, Korea, this church still stands unharmed. Crewmen of the 2nd Platoon, Heavy Mortar Company, 32nd RCT fire on enemy held hill near Ami-Dong. Small arms fire was holding up advancing 7th Infantry Division. Burst can be seen near summit on hill.

1 Mar 1951

Cold GIs Moving Up - Warmly clad, but still cold
infantrymen of the 7th Inf Div advances against the
enemy near Hadaewa Korea. Many of them still clad in
the old GI boots and lacked winter arctic boots. The scene
looks like a Willie & Joe cartoon of infantrymen in WWII.
When I talked to various troops I never heard them
complain about the weather. We had a job to do and we
did it!

Two soldiers
with Company
"G" 17th RCT
stay low as
climbing near
Kumma-Ri.

Enemy burp guns opened up when they were about
three quarters of the way up. The 7th Inf. Div. artillery
opened up later and the hill was taken by us shortly
after.   19 Feb 51

323

FOOT BRIDGE RIVER ICED - GIs of the 7th Infantry Division, "Light Company, 32nd RCT cross a river south of PARGCHPO over a footbridge erected by the unit's 13th Combat Engineers. Without the bridge, the men would have had to wade across the ice caked river, in this zero weather. This could have resulted in cases of foot frostbite.   13 March 1951

These men of Company "L", 32nd RCT, 7th Inf Div, try to find dry footing as they cross an icy river. UN troops continued their assault against the fleeing Chinese forces. The GIs were advancing too fast to wait for the 13th Combat Engineers to erect a new span. This was south of PAEGCHPO-RI. 13 March 1951

Heading for mountains and the enemy lines. We are moving up safely which is why we are marching close as the enemy moved back. Our vehicles could not move up because of the snow so we marched by foot.

Men of "E" Company, 17th RCT advancing toward Hill 675 near Kumma-Ri in Korea pass a dead North Korean Soldier armed with an M-1 rifle and ammunition.
The men were clad in winter gear that the Quartermaster issued to them recently. They are smart soldiers, very well apart from one another to evade any enemy incoming fire.   20 Feb. 1951

My left shoe
shows up on
the lower right
of the photo.
While climbing
up to the
summit of the
hill, the enemy
sprayed us
with gunfire.
No one got hit
and we topped
it soon.
1950

A Quad 50 Cal Track & Truck slid off icy mountain pass, 3 GIs hurt.   The 7th Inf. Div. had a few vehicles slip on other icy roads

RECOILS RIFLE TEAM - On a windy and freezing day, a 57MM recoilless rifle team from "E" Company, 17th RCT walk down a snow covered hillside slope, in their advance. This 7th Inf Div unit was on the way to their target, Hill 675 near Kumma-Ri in Korea. The men were clad in winter gear that Quartermaster issued to them recently.   20 Feb. 1951

ROK and American soldiers of the 17th RCT7th Inf Division move along a snowy mountain road as they advance towards enemy held positions northeast of Pyongchang, Korea. They are not spread more apart as our planes did not spot the enemy in their advance.   7 Mar 1951

Staying in the tree line on the mountain, troops move up to surprise enemy on hills ahead.

Sgt. James E Ward (Nahma, MI) gunner with the 32nd heavy tank co, 7th Infantry Division, watches as the navy and marine fighter-bombers strafe enemy-held hill on edge of the village of Yonhwa-Dong, Korea.
24 April 1951

Stretching as far as the eyes could see, this convoy of the 7th Infantry Division, Ordnance Battalion moves along mountain roads, transporting tons of needed supplies to division units under heavy attack by the communist enemy.

Front line units always thanked ordnance supply vehicles when their vehicles showed up.

Spring 1951

Crossing Korean rivers in sub zero temperature can be very dangerous. Besides enemy fire, the freezing elements can inflict serious losses on advancing Allied troops. In many cases, the enemy had opened dams and ankle deep river crossings became waist deep-water medical problems. This has led to frost bite and shock, plus limiting the size of assault teams in assaults.

This narrow and cold stream, shallow as it is, is having a footbridge constructed by enlisted men of the 7th Infantry Division team of 13th Combat Engineer Battalion. Troops waiting to cross will now have dry feet and cut down on medical assistance. The GIs are near the town of Talmorisil.

28 Feb. 1951

YALU RIVER

Yalu River

Two enlisted men of the 7th Signal Company gaze across the
cold, frozen Yalu River at the mountains of Manchuria and
the small village just below. Cpl. Murphy, a photo lab
technician and Cpl. Wilfred Hunkins, a combat photographer were among the first GIs to reach the border town
of Hyesanjin. Cpt. John Murphy is a lab technician and Cpt.
Wilfred Hunkins (San Francisco, Cal.) is a Combat still
photographer with the unit.

A bridge set aflame by the Air Force burns. The only signs
of humanity were two Chinese Soldiers walking on the
northern banks of the river in Manchuria, at the edge of
the village. The 17th Infantry Regiment of the 7th Infantry
Division was the first and only American combat unit to
reach the Manchurian border.

To the left of the GIs can be smoke rising from a wooden
bridge that leads into Manchuria. The temple on the left
was not damaged at all by air or ground fire. Walking on
the ice and snow, near the edge of the river and passing the
hamlet were two well clad Chinese soldiers; to protect them
from the severe cold. Other people were seen at the time.
Cpl. Hunkins was in the group of the first ten American
soldiers to reach the border.   **21 Nov. 1950**

Yalu REACHING RIVER

The first two Americans to reach the Manchurian border and the Yalu River, stop to relax and have their photograph taken. CPL. Mayford J. Gardner (L) from Royal Oak, Michigan and PFC Tommie L. Robinson of Las Cruces, New Mexico.

The "point men" for the advance were alert in the final drive; watching out for snipers, enemy activity or mines. Freezing as they were, they were happy to be the first to the river.   Both are with the 17th Infantry Regiment.

21 November 1950

REACHING Yalu RIVER - 1ˢᵀ 2 GIs TO RIVER - The first three men to reach the border of the Yalu River, at Hyeanjin, Korea, pause to rest during their advance against the communist forces.

L-R Sgt. Peter Ruplenas (South Boston, Mass) still photographer ASGD to the 7ᵗʰ Infantry Division; Cpl. Mayford Gardner (Royal Oak, MI); and PFC Tommie Robinson (Las Cruces, NM)

Gardner and Robinson were point men with the 7ᵗʰ Inf. Div. and led them first. Photo by Hunkins   21 Nov 1950

Family-November 16, 1970

Yalu River - shot after the 17th RCT, 7th Infantry Division secured the town of HYSEN-JIN in North Korea, the "brass" arrived for a formal picture. Not looking out over the banks of the river towards Manchuria, but facing the combat troops in Korea that secured the town, the leaders relax as they thought this would expedite final victory.

(L to R) Brig. Gen. Homer Kiefer, CG 7th Div. Artillery; Brig. Gen. Henry I Hodes, Asst. CG X Corps; Maj. Gen. Edward M. Almond, CG X Corps: Maj. Gen. David G. Barr, CG 7th Infantry Division and Col. Herbert B. Powell whose 17th RCT men were the first Americans to reach the Manchurian border.

When Colonel Powell reached the river he said "The hell with the gooks" and spit in the river. Then he proceeded to urinate in the river in disrespect. I followed him as any good soldier would.

21 November 1950

Taken on the ice of the Yalu River, with Manchuria in the rear ... Taken on the ice of the Yalu River, with Manchuria in the rear ... tographers take a break. (l to r) Cpl. Wilfred Hunkins ... Popienas. 'Ole Man Rupy' was the first ... first ten men to reach ...

To Mom & Dad:
All the best love in
the world from way up here
on the Manchurian border.
Nov. 21, 1950 "Pete"

THURSDAY, FEBRUARY 8, 1951

(U. S. Army Photo)

BOSTON MAN ON YALU RIVER — Sgt Peter P. Ruplenas, son of Mr. and Mrs. John Reulenas, 427 East 6th st., South Boston, looks across border from Korea into Manchuria. An Army combat photographer, Ruplenas was third man to reach the river boundary. He followed two infantry scouts. He is expecting the arrival of a new member of the family. His wife, Hazel, is at Sendai, Japan.

I was the 3rd American to reach the banks of the Yalu river in North Korea; posing on the Korean side of the river as abandoned houses in Manchuria, China show in background. I was a still and cinematographer with the 7th Signal Company and followed two 17th regiment point men to the frozen Yalu River to photograph their trip.

Much later, after everything was secures, the civilian news media arrived to conduct interviews and pose GIs on the banks.   21 Nov 1950

339

REUNIONS
and
MEMORIALS

Observation Post 211 Manned by 1ˢᵗ Reconnaissance Squadron 9ᵗʰ Cavalry

Military Statue in Malaysia

486th Bomb
Group Reunion

**At one of our DASPO reunions we visited the
Korean War Memorial in Washington DC**

A few years back we flew to Boston to visit my brother who is now 97. We went for a ride to Cape Cod where we met a Veteran from the Korean War.

Hyannis Korean War Memorial

Meeting other Veterans at the Korean War Rededication Washington DC

TRIBUTES

A Word from " Rupy"

In the past my son, John, has conned me into going to Los Angeles and then renting a car to go to Las Vegas which we did. We went to a Korean War Reunion and on my Birthday somehow I met Elvis decades after his... "death". Well

"THE KING" sang me Happy Birthday a few other songs and his American Trilogy. Then a giant Birthday cake was rolled in, and Elvis gave me his sunglasses. John did not read the verse in the Good Book about lying or honoring thy Father because I have a hard time believing that this was an accident or the next story that follows an accident. But bless his heart at least he means well.

This March, 2014, we were both tired of the snow and somehow I "won" 2 tickets for a Caribbean cruise and that was fine with me because this past winter was brutal. Little did I know he lied to me (WHAT?!? He never lies!) and a small boat ride on St. Martin turned into an adventure, a parasailing adventure. Of course he had the chance of going 400, 600 or 800 feet. What do you suppose he did?

Check it out at YOU TUBE:
https://www.youtube.com/watch?v=AOB_7Bri1h8

Christel Horst is the lady in the photo with my photo and certificate, proving that I did indeed parasail!

HERE ARE A FEW COMMENTS BY MY FRIENDS

Thanks to all! My son also runs a Facebook page for me; just look up my name Peter P. Ruplenas. Some I know, some I do not, thank you to all and God Bless America and ALL Veterans!

The following are comments which my Facebook friends said about me and I thank them all!

This is a man who had to leave his B-17 bomber in a hurry and parachute into Nazi-occupied Europe. Should anyone be surprised that, 70 years later, he's parasailing? Way to go, Rupy!!!
---   *Edward Ahrens*

Way to go Rupy. You probably have not had that much fun since Vietnam.   Roger B. Hawkins

Rhonda Druell Rodriguez - That's awesome!!'

Autumn Henderson - looks like you had a great time Rupy!

Chambers Custom -- Enjoyin' life! Way to go Rupy!

Michael Baker Outstanding. Carpe Diem. - You are still my hero.

Kit Kramer   - Outstanding! God bless. The Greatest Generation still blazing new trails.

Robert Renner - Awesome!!!

When you survive three wars, it's amazing how many fellow veterans you can find! Thank you for your (repeated) service to our country! --- Edward Ahrens

"It was an honor to have Peter "Rupy" Ruplenas as Grand Marshal of the 2013 Brunswick Veterans Day Parade. I was charmed by Rupy's wit and humble demeanor. I am so pleased to have met him and see his photographs from WWII which are etched in my memory." --- Fay M. Kaufman Brunswick Veterans ParadeCity of Brunswick, MD

Today, I received your book, 2 Cameras 3 Wars WWII Edition-- wow!!! I look forward to reading it; have already, perused. I salute your dedication and service to our country!

I wasn't a DASPO member, but was honored to meet your father and hear of his experiences. As a USAF Gunship Crew Member we flew with a Combat Photographer so am familiar with the important product they provide, in our case it supported the mission we flew and verified our mission results.

I first met Rupy at a train show in Brunswick Maryland, Oct 2013. As a train club member I was helping run an American Flyer Layout on display at the town's annual Railroad Festival. I saw Rupy admiring one of my steam engines as it made its circuit. As a veteran I noted his shirt with his military medals (especially his purple heart), ribbons, and patches and asked him what he did in the Army. When he said he had been a photographer in three wars I told him that if Vietnam I was an AC-130 Gunner and our Gunship crew included a combat photographer position. I appreciated that combat photographers endured the same risks and danger that as other combat aircrew members. I also appreciated that I had only one war in my case and he had gone through three!

I was honored to meet and talk with Rupy about his experiences and thank him for his distinguished service to our country.

Joe Glenn, Captain USAF (Ret)   AC-130 Spectre Gunner

I was in DASPO 1967-69. Any one who met Rupy was blessed. He was willing to help and teach new photographers like my self. He always encouraged everyone in the unit which is one reason why DASPO was the best photo unit in the U.S. Army. His sense of humor was next to none. I was glad to know and serve with Him even if only for a short time.   --- Craig Fairall

I was a 84C/84B army cameraman from 1961-1973. I had the great privilege to serve with SFC Pete Ruplenas, forever known as Rupy, at DASPO PAC out of Ft. Shafter, Hawaii, from 1965-1967. Not merely to serve with him but to count he and his wife Helen as friends.

I remember Pete as a proud soldier, dedicated to the mission, always ready to share his knowledge with the younger men. I also remember a warm, friendly, family man with a marvelous sense of humor.

God bless, Rupy.   - SSG Kit D. Kramer

John

What I remember about Rupy is his smile. He was grumpy some days but it's the smile I remember and he was always willing to help you with your photo techniques. His stories were like listening to someone narrating a history film. You could close your eyes and see everything he described. I was never fortunate to get to go into the field with Rupy, that I regret. He was a great guy to always be around.

Jerry Hains (DASPO 67-69)

Pete Ruplenas was my sergeant, my NCOIC on several jobs, a regular, good guy who took me into his home many times to share family meals with his wife and sons. He taught me about photography, about the Army and about how the Army operated and what the Army expected, photographically, and otherwise. Pete is an ornery, opinionated and talented man. He's a good friend and his age belies his zest for life and fun. You meet people in your journey through life and remember few and forget many. Pete Ruplenas has always stayed in my mind. He shared his gifts with young guys who cared enough to linger with him and I'm ever grateful for that. God Bless him for his service to our country over three wars and so many years.
Sincerely, Jim Egan

COMBAT PHOTOGRAPHY

By definition war photography captures photographs of armed conflict and life in war-torn areas. The first known photographer was a surgeon named John McCosh, 1848 – 1849 serving in the Bengal Army during the Second Sihk War. The British established war photography during the Crimean War in 1854.

At first the photography was used as a systemic coverage of war for the benefit of the public. The coverage focused or depicted the dignified aspects of war and then later showed the destruction and aftermath. The American Civil War is a great example of the latter and it is here where photographers went to great lengths in recreating scenes of battle designed to intensify the visual and emotional effects of battle.

Moving into and through the 20th century, war photographers have covered all major conflicts and many were killed. Today you will find them still placed in harm's way and sometimes killed trying to get their pictures out of the war arena. They are protected by international laws but, it has become even more dangerous with the advent of terrorism.

Combat Photographers are a unique, brave, daring, and special breed of people in our uniformed service. In fact to be on the ground with the "ground pounders" and sharing with them the brutality, shock, and realism of life in the maw of raw hell known as combat, armed only with cameras, film, and a side arm makes them a special breed of people in deed.

Respectfully, Brian P. McDermott USMC (Capt)

Glad to hear Pete is doing better. Pete was one of my heroes as well as a dear friend. Vietnam was his third war as a combat cameraman. When others went into battle with weapons we went with cameras. When they shot bullets we shot film. It takes a special kind of person to do that and Pete did it for three wars. --- Kit Kramer

Hello John,

Thank you for the update on your father. I am so happy to hear that he is getting better. My continued thoughts and prayers for him will be going his way. Please keep me posted if you would.

I am also happy to hear of his second book coming out. The pictures in his first book are very moving. I have not had the privilege of meeting your father face to face. I cannot even put into words the respect I have for him. It is men like your father that are the core of what makes this country great.

I would like to say to your father: Mr Ruplenas, you sir are a great man. It is men like you that showed extreme bravery and dedication to country that make this nation great. Your work and photographs are truly amazing. I cannot express enough my gratitude for all you have given. It is an honor and privilege to know you.   ---Robert B Renner

If there is anything I can be of assistance with please let me know. I wish you and your family all the best. Please take good care of your father. Thoughts and prayers going out to you all. Thanks again.   Robert "Big Bear" Renner

God bless those that sacrifice for their country.

God bless those who sacrifice time with loved ones in the home and in exchange receive the animosity of our enemies. God bless those who sacrifice the comfort we have been blessed with in our county, enduring the horrible conditions of war. And God bless those who sacrifice safety, which we enjoy, going into the line of fire, and oftentimes losing life and limb.

May God bless them, for they sacrifice, in love, for their families, for their friends, and for their country.Jesus deserves the last word- on what it means to love, and what it means to serve- and these seen clearly in those who serve willingly in the armed forces of our country.

Chris Korcsmaros

"Greater love has no one than this: to lay down one's life for one's friends." --- John 15:13

Being a photographer for 33 years, and a Vietnam veteran, I took an instant liking to Peter. I have a slight inkling of what Peter experienced when I was shot at in Vietnam and in Gaza. I hope he lives long and happy. --- Ken Owens

As your Dad use to say about my captions: "Lafoon, your Engwish ain't worth a damn". So, feel free to make corrections.

I got to the unit in Sep 65. I'm not sure of the actual month you all arrived. Tell the "Old Bastard" I said hi and hope he is doing great. --- Bob Lafoon

When my son is not busy conning me into misguided adventures I like to relax with my Birthday present last year... my Shih Tzu dog Bobi.
Bobi does not con me into doing anything unlike some people!

...and there's more

I would like to take a moment to introduce you all to a TRUE American hero, and he's right here on *my* friends list!
About 2 years ago I had an assignment in one of my classes which required me to find a war photographer and discuss his technique and images. At the time I was residing at the home of one such person, but none of his photos were available online for use.
So I asked him if he knew if any of his buddies could fill the position and he told me about "Rupy". --- Autumn Henderson

Jen Garland Waters -- That is awesome!!

Kathy Cheatham
 How wonderful that someone like this had the courage to stand behind that camera during wartime. Pretty amazing.
Thanks for contributing a picture to history Rupy. Those pictures are the things that never let us forget.

Susan N Sunshine
 Through your photography work, you have brought these wars into our homes; thank you for sharing your up-close & personal moments in time, & thank you, Mr. Ruplenas, for your service. We are a free & proud country because of men, & women, such as yourself. You, sir, have my utmost respect.

Mary Gordon - too cool!!! he's adorable!!

Chuck Dezarn   - Very cool...

Craig Bailey - Awesome, God bless you Ruby

Chadley Alsip - Thank you for your services sir ... god bless ...

JR Swindell III - Thank you sir for documenting our heroes, and acting heroically yourself...you have successfully preserved the truth
of war for future generations. God bless you sir, you have my honor and respect.

Jeff Bonnell - thank you sir !!

Zig Zag - WOW! this is awesome! He could have taken pictures of any one of four of my relatives who fought in two of those wars.

Zig Zag - this is my camera this is my gun this ones for snapshots so I better run!

Melanie Smith Leachman - Very Cool!

I do not know him personally but only thru FB. But I am a combat veteran, 48 months in the Middle East as an Infantrymen and I have known a combat photographer or 2 and I have loads of respect for them.
Even more so for your father for all that he has endured, it has been my utmost honor to have gotten to know him over the last 6 months through FB.
Daily I look forward to both updates and to see how he is doing. Men like Peter Ruplenas should he honored for all time.
--- SGT James Cunningham(RET)

Roger B. Hawkins
Thanks for the update. I have talked to him on the phone, but never in person. My DASPO time was in the Pentagon. But I know the legend and wish him the best. I have some fel for what he has been through. While in the ICU after dual knee replacement I had hypercapnic lung failure which required an emergency team to get me started again. So we are recovering together. Give Pete a double thumbs up from me.

John, I have never had the pleasure of meeting you father. We became friends on Facebook because I was fascinated by his military record. While Pete and I both served in Vietnam, I was particularly interested in his missions over Europe with the 8th Air Force. As a student of history, I deeply appreciate the contributions of combat photographers. Thanks, Ed Ahrens

Lisa King -- Pretty awesome! Bless you Rupy!!

My Friend Pete

Shortly after I moved from Maryland to West Virginia in January of 2007, I had the privilege of meeting my elderly neighbor, Peter Replenas. I was amazed at how vibrant and healthy Pete was for being in his 90's.

Tom Bowers and Rupy

I tell people, "give that man a shopping cart, and I can't keep up with him!" It did not take me long to learn to love this man. His wit is sharp as a tack, and his memories are vivid with detail. I quickly learned of the many trials this man went through during his many years on this planet, and I have gained the utmost respect for him.

His beginnings were humble. He was a child of immigrant parents who came to the United States of America to make a better life for themselves and their They worked hard, and instilled that work ethic in Pete. Prior to the outbreak of World War II, Pete enlisted in the United States Army and became a combat photographer.
He loved the regimented life and made the military his first career. He served in the European Theatre during the WWII, then served in Korea, and Vietnam. Many of his photographs are published in many books. He loved his work, and would place himself in mortal danger to capture history and show the world what the American soldier had to endure during their service for their country. He lost friends in war, and tears welt up in his eyes to this day when he speaks of them.

Life has not been a cake walk for Pete. Not only has he lost his wife of many years, but he also lost a son. He has been shot, suffered frostbite, and his eyes have seen so much horror, suffering, and death. Yet, when you sit down and talk with this honorable man, he often says he has been blessed in life. It does not take much to make Pete smile and I love to hear him share his memories. This man does not have a mean bone in his frail body, and I feel blessed that he has called me his friend. I salute my friend, "Pete."